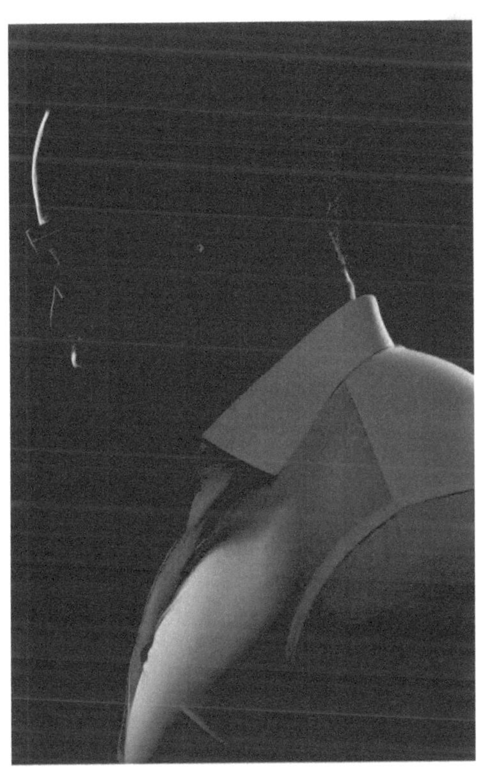

# Dream. Walk. Live.

Mac Harvey

Oceanfront Press—Miami, FL
ISBN: 979-8-218-17649-5
Library of Congress Control Number: 2023905438
Title: *Dream. Walk. Live.*
Author: Mac Harvey
Digital distribution | 2023
Paperback | 2023

# Dedication

This book is dedicated to my late father, who instilled in me a love for learning and a passion for achieving greatness. Although you are no longer with us, your spirit lives on in the pursuit of my dreams, and I am forever grateful for the love and guidance you provided.

To my mother, who has always been my rock and my source of strength. Your unwavering support and encouragement have been invaluable to me, and I could not have achieved my goals without you.

To my grandmother, who sacrificed so much to help me achieve my dreams. Your tireless efforts, including recycling soda cans to save money for me to go to college, will never be forgotten, and I am forever grateful for your love and dedication.

To my uncle, who inspired me to be the best in my craft. Your guidance and mentorship have been instrumental in shaping my career, and I am honored to call you my family.

To all my wonderful friends who have inspired me to be the best version of myself. Your love, support, and encouragement have been a constant source of inspiration, and I am grateful for the role you have played in my life.

This book is dedicated to all of you, who have played a significant role in shaping who I am today. Thank you for your love, support, and encouragement, and for believing in me even when I didn't believe in myself. This is for you.

# Table of Contents

# Chapter 1

Growing up in a small town in southwest Virginia, we call it the New River Valley. In my town, it was so small we didn't even have a traffic light we had two convenience stores and the post office. Imagine living in an existence where people blow the car horn and they're being friendly and saying hi.

Before I was born my parents also grew up in the same parts of Virginia, my mother and I graduated from the same high school. My mother and father met and my grandfather's funeral, what an interesting place to get a girl's phone number. It turns out that my father's baby sister and my mom were good friends. Six weeks later my parents eloped, and it's been a happy 30-year love story of them being together.

In the magical year of 1982, the year Michael Jackson releases Thriller my favorite all-time album, I was born they named me Max. It was quite a very magical experience being an only child raised by my parents, grandparents, and aunt. We all lived in the same house, full of love and laughter jokes, and musical talent. My mother was the singer, my aunt, and my grandmother played the piano at our church next door and here I am just a baby taking it all in. When family and friends used to come to visit everyone wanted to hold me.

I used to love watching my family cook in the kitchen, I would see my grandmother sitting by the dining room table peeling potatoes. She was saying just an amazing character to witness she couldn't see well but she could walk all over the house and knew where everything was. She could tell by your footsteps who the person was when you entered the room, and she automatically knew when my baby steps were anywhere around her. My family cooked such amazing food it's no wonder we never hardly ever ate out. In the mornings you could smell those eggs, bacon, and biscuits, from a mile away warm and buttered. My mother would always cook for my father before he left for work and then she would cook for me. I used to love it when my mother put apple butter on my biscuit and then she'd make me some eggs and fried apples. Yes, we are southern country folks and proud of it. We don't call it a "Wash Cloth," we call it a "Wash Rag." We don't say "Diabetes," we say you got the "Sugars."

My family was all about acts of service that's how we showed our love to one another whether it was through cooking, we would always do for one another. It was a very giving existence, and I love that. I used to love going outside and seeing my grandparents my grandfather would be working in the garden and sometimes my grandmother would sit on the porch with her fly swatter trying to keep the flies out of the house. I would always be running in and out of the house, so my grandmother would say "stay in or stay out you're letting the flies in." I used to love watching my father ride the tractor and mow the grass. We lived on a hill next to the New River by the railroad tracks, so it was such a calm beautiful, serene place to grow up. We loved the sound of birds singing in the morning and crickets at night. There were no streetlights so when it was nighttime it was dark, perfect for hide-n-seek. It planted seeds in the back of my mind if it's beautiful like this here what does the rest of the world look like?

My family was very religious, the church I grew up in was next door. My family had me in Sunday school every Sunday. That's when I first learned about other places in the world like Jerusalem and Israel. I was like wow in my mind when I first heard the Red Sea. I was intrigued I was like the sea is red I can't wait to see that. Hearing about all the stories in the Bible, I was like wow my imagination was running wild with me trying to see what it would be like to walk on water.

My family and I would always take part in a Christmas play every year and they were quite comical. One year my mom and father played Mary and Joseph. My mom was the perfect Mary kind, gentle, and poise. She carried the role with grace and reverence. My father, on the other hand, was a bit too hyperactive for the role. He strutted around the stage with all the gusto of a professional thespian. Everyone got a good laugh as he stumbled through his lines, often forgetting them in the process.

My mom was quick to pick up the slack and would whisper his lines to him from the side of the stage. My father would then repeat them with an exaggerated, overly dramatic flair. The audience was in stitches by the end of the play.

Growing up with my father was an amazing experience because he was truly a nomad before he met my mother. Some of the stories he would tell me of where he lived like Columbus OH and Detroit MI. He loved to take road trips it was so amazing. One of my favorite road trips growing up my father brought a new car and was so eager to get it on the road. We took a family trip from Virginia to Disney World in Orlando Florida. Another one of my other favorite road trips was on Independence Day weekend we drove to Chicago, and we were huge Michael Jordan fans. My father took us to Michael Jordan's restaurant I was hoping and crossing my fingers that maybe Michael's in town and he'd walk in and I'd see him. We did go to the United Center and saw the statue of Michael Jordan. This was the time I realize I wanted to learn more about the world as a kid.

In the early years of growing up my family didn't have cable television we only had three channels. Eventually, we got satellite which opened a whole new demystified world of all the channels that you could watch.

I was intrigued the first time me watching Nickelodeon as a kid. Then on one Saturday afternoon stumbled upon the Travel Channel. I was in absolute amazement I used to watch this show called Passport to Europe with Samantha Brown and she would go to all these cool places around the world. I was like this is exactly what I wanted to do. My family didn't have passports for us to travel, it was a very humbling existence growing up we had everything we ever needed. I had asked my father if we could take a trip overseas. My father didn't want to say we didn't have the money at the time so my father came up with one of the best solutions that a father could come up with.

He takes my mom and I to New York City and my father said this city you can go around the world on one island. He was right I was completely enthralled as I was walking around with my family seeing so many different cultures and they all look different speaking different languages and dialects. We never had Italian food in my small town or Greek food or Chinese. In my small town, we couldn't even get pizza delivery. I always appreciate my father for challenging my mindset and showing me there's so much more to see than where we are.

Road trips were just our thing, we never took a plane my entire childhood. I appreciated it so much because you get to see so much and look out the window when you're going places and that taught me about the importance of enjoying the journey as well as the destination.

My father and I had a special bond, forged on the open road as we explored the countryside together. Every summer, we would pack up the car and set out on a new adventure, each one more exciting than the last.

As we drove through rolling hills and across sun-dappled fields, my father would remind me of his travels and the people he had met along the way. He had a way of making every story come to life, bringing characters to life with his vivid descriptions and infectious laughter.

I was fascinated by the world and its endless possibilities; every mile we covered only fueled my imagination further. My father was always encouraging, pushing me to learn more about the world and never be afraid to try something new.

As we stopped at dusty diners and tiny mom-and-pop shops along the way, I learned that life was about the people you meet and the memories you made along the way.

As a kid, I had so much joy and fulfillment with the little excursions that I would do with my family. Once a month we would all take a family trip to the grocery store I used to love running up and down the aisles grabbing certain things and sneaking it into the cart. Quite amazing that we could go to the grocery store and buy enough food for the entire family, and it would last us a whole month.

Most Saturday afternoons, I spent time with my grandfather, we would watch wrestling we were huge fans of Ric Flair and Hulk Hogan. Afterward, he would take me outside and I didn't realize at the moment as a kid just how talented my grandfather truly was, he would collect popsicle sticks and he could build little houses with them he was like a little architect and an engineer.

My grandfather built the house I grew up in with his own hands. It was a five-bedroom house, one bath several acres of land. Just watching him walk around the building and fix things was incredible. Father and grandfather, I marveled at them like they were superhuman just old school strong broad shoulder-tall kind of men that you go to them, and you just tell them something's broken they could fix anything. He and my father weren't scared of anything I remember there was a mouse that was in the house. They didn't mind getting their hands dirty but when it came time to dress up. My father and Grandfather were very dapper in their suits, and they taught me about taking pride in your appearance. My mom, grandmother, and aunt were mortified they were standing on chairs yelling for my grandfather or my father to come to get it. They would just walk nonchalantly into the house completely fearless at the situation catch the mouse and go back outside and handle business. So, there were times I would ride with him to the hardware store. My grandfather had the coolest pickup truck it was a classic royal blue 1964 Ford pickup everybody knew it was my grandfather just by the pickup truck.

He always had a smile on his face and a joke to tell, even when things got tough. I remember when I was about eight or nine years old, my grandfather had to have surgery, and I was so worried about him. I remember sitting by his bedside as he recovered and promised myself that I would always take care of him.

When my grandfather was better, he would take me on adventures all over the countryside, showing me all the hidden gems of Southwest Virginia. We would fish in the streams, hunt in the woods, and explore the caves and hills. I learned so much from my grandfather about nature and about life. He taught me about hard work and perseverance, and I learned that no matter what, family is always there to support you.

My neighbors are my cousins, it was like having a family reunion all year round. I just love watching my family interact and how they showed each other love. Growing up I rarely ever saw family conflicts and when I look back on it as an adult I was like wow. I also had another neighbor that was a family friend he had a ranch and sometimes the horses would get out and they'd run around our yard it was so cool. At times he would host rodeos and I'd go up there and watch a rodeo.

I loved visiting my neighbor's ranch and watching the horses run wild. It was an experience unlike any other and I felt like a cowboy right alongside him. The rodeos he hosted were exciting and gave me a taste of the wild west. It was amazing to see the skill and bravery of the riders as they competed in various events like bull riding and barrel racing.

But the most important lesson I learned from my neighbor was the importance of hard work and dedication. He worked tirelessly on his ranch every day and seeing his dedication taught me that success comes from putting in the effort. He also taught me about the importance of taking care of the land and animals, and how that responsibility came with great rewards.

It was a beautiful sweet innocent existence; Life just seems so simple my family taught me so much about how to appreciate the simple things. I used to love waking up every morning and hearing the sound of the train going by. I would look out of my bedroom window, and I could see the river and some people in my town going fishing early in the morning.

The people who lived there are proud of our roots, and many have lived in the area for generations. A lot of close-knit groups of families looked out for one another and took care of each other.

Life in Southwest Virginia was simple yet fulfilling. The rolling hills and lush forests provided a breathtaking backdrop to daily life, and the residents enjoy spending time outdoors, fishing, hunting, and exploring the land.

The community was built around the coal mines, and many of the residents worked in the mines, related industries, or in education. Despite the hard work, so many take great pride in our jobs and in the role they played in providing energy to the rest of the country.

In the evenings, the residents would gather at the local diner to share stories and catch up on the latest news. We could sit for hours, drinking coffee and laughing, and nobody ever seemed to be in a hurry to leave.

Our community is tight-knit, and everyone took care of one another. When someone was in need, whether it was a sick child or a family going through tough times, the entire community would come together to help.

Despite the challenges that came with living in a rural area, the people of Southwest Virginia are happy and content. Each of us cherished our way of life and was grateful for the beauty of the land and the tight-knit community they called home.

# Chapter 2

As an only child, there were pros and cons, and sometimes I wished I had a sibling. My friends were jealous of me because they said, "you don't have to share anything."

Even though I had my little cousin living on the hill, it still felt different. I internalized a lot and didn't share many things that were going on with me because I didn't feel like my parents could relate. It became a habit for me to just deal with it on my own.

On Saturday mornings, I used to love waking up and turning on the TV to watch cartoons. The Muppet Babies and Teenage Mutant Ninja Turtles were my favorite cartoons. As a child, I was goofy and nerdy. I would trip over my own two feet if I wasn't careful. During the week, I used to hate waking up early in the morning to get ready for school. When there was bad weather, I would turn on the TV and look for my school at the bottom of the news to see if we were opening two hours late or if we were closed.

At the beginning of every school year, my father would always buy me the latest new Jordan sneakers that just hit the market. I couldn't wait to get over to the mall to pick them up. On the first day of school, I would lay my clothes out on the bed with my shoes. I didn't even allow my shoes to touch the floor.

The most wonderful time of the year is my birthday! Every year, my mom went above and beyond to make my special day extra memorable. Whether it was having a magical unicorn-themed party or a pool party at our local community center, each event was the highlight of my summer.

My mom was an expert party planner, ensuring that there was something for everyone. She always made the most exquisite cakes in a variety of flavors from chocolate to vanilla. She also set up an array of fun activities, such as balloon fights and scavenger hunts. No matter what the theme was, she always made sure that everyone had a blast.

The best part of my mom's parties was always the ending. We'd all gather around the cake, blow out the candles, and celebrate my birthday. Everyone, even my friends, would sing "Happy Birthday" to me, and my mom would give me a special present. I was always so happy and thankful to everyone who made my special day even more special.

Cooking Memories

I have so many fond memories of spending time in the kitchen with my mother and grandmother, cooking and baking delicious meals together. They taught me how to make a variety of dishes, including Meatloaf, Pot Roast, Sloppy Joes, and Stuffed Peppers.

Every meal was cooked with love and attention to detail, and you could always smell the delicious aromas wafting from the kitchen. The meatloaf was savory and moist, and the pot roast was tender and flavorful. The Sloppy Joes were messy but delicious, and the stuffed peppers were filled with a hearty mixture of rice, ground beef, and spices.

To accompany the main dishes, I learned to make side dishes like Corn Pudding, Baked Beans, Mashed Potatoes, and Gravy. The Corn Pudding was sweet and creamy, the baked beans were tangy and smoky, and the mashed potatoes were light and fluffy. The gravy was rich and savory, the perfect finishing touch to the meal.

For dessert, my family indulged in sweet treats like Cherry Cheesecake, Pound Cake, and Chocolate Cake. The cherry cheesecake was tangy and creamy, the pound cake was dense and buttery, and the chocolate cake was rich and indulgent.

Going to Vacation Bible School every summer was such a blast for me and my cousins. I was so excited to be there, and I was sure I was going to learn all about the Bible.

Little did I know that Vacation Bible School was going to be a lot different than I expected. On the first day, I was assigned to the group with the most energetic teacher, the one in charge of the arts-and-crafts room. I soon found out that instead of learning about Jesus and the Bible, we were making paper crosses and papier-mâché animals. On the second day, I was in the music room, which was even more chaotic. Instead of singing hymns, our teacher was teaching us dance moves to popular pop songs. I had never seen anything like it before, and I felt so out of place.

On the last day, I was in the drama room. We had to act out Bible stories, but instead of using props and costumes, we had to act out the stories with our bodies and voices. I must say, I was pretty good at it, and my teacher praised me for my performance.

Looking back, I can now laugh at my experiences at Vacation Bible School. It was different than I expected, and I am thankful that I had the chance to have those crazy experiences.

Summer break was always a blast, except for that one time I went to the pool with my father. It was a sunny hot day, and I had decided to go for a swim. I dove in without thinking and quickly found myself way over my head, as I had miscalculated how deep the water was.

I was thrashing around, desperately trying to reach the surface, but the more I moved, the more energy I wasted. I started to panic, struggling to stay above the surface, when suddenly I felt something strong brush against my leg. I stopped struggling, terrified of what it could be. It was then that I realized that it was my father. He had seen me in trouble and dived in to save me. With a few powerful strokes, he managed to reach me and pull me back to safety.

That moment of terror, when I thought, I was going to drown, will stay with me forever. I was incredibly lucky to have my father there to save me. To this day, I'm eternally grateful to him for being there when I needed him most.

I loved all kinds of music growing up, whether it was Aaliyah, Dave Matthews Band, Red Hot Chili Peppers, or TLC. As long as it sounded good, I could easily vibe to it. I used to love watching Fresh Prince of Bel-Air with the family every Monday night when it would air on NBC. Afterwards, my mom would send me off to bed; she didn't want me up late. As I grew older, I related so much to Carlton from the show because he was a smart nerd, and I was too, just bigger and taller.

## First Concert

I finally got permission from my parents to go to a concert. They got my friend Brandon and I tickets and we are big fans of hip-hop music, and one of your favorite artists was Busta Rhymes. When we heard that he was going to be performing at Virginia Tech, I was so thrilled. My father was just as excited to drive us to see the concert.

We both arrived at the venue early and got a good spot near the stage. We were surrounded by thousands of other fans, all eagerly waiting for the show to start. When the lights went down, the crowd erupted into cheers and applause, and I felt a rush of excitement.

Busta Rhymes took the stage, and the energy in the room was electric. He started the show with one of his biggest hits, and the atmosphere went wild. Brandon and I were dancing and rapping along to every song, and we felt like you were part of something special.

The concert was a blur of lights, music, and excitement. Busta Rhymes was a master showman, and he had the crowd in the palm of his hand. He performed for over an hour, and we both were exhausted but exhilarated when the show finally came to an end.

After that concert I was so elated I was researching who is the next artist that was coming near my hometown because I just love being part of that kind of energy.

My father picks me up from school and I had mentioned that there was a Bad Boy tour that was coming to Roanoke VA. He surprised me with tickets to go I was in absolute shock and the concert was that night. I was so excited I didn't even want to go home shower and change clothes I wanted to go straight there.

As we arrived there were thousands of people filled the Roanoke Civic Center to watch the Bad Boy Records tour. Puff Daddy and Mase headlined the show and paid tribute to the recently deceased Notorious BIG.

As the lights dimmed and the crowd erupted in cheers, Puff Daddy and Mase came out, starting with Puff Daddy's hit single "Can't Nobody Hold Me Down." The entire arena was filled with energy, and the music was so loud that it could be heard outside of the arena.

Mase then performed his hit single "Been Around the World," the crowd singing along to every word. Puff Daddy and Mase had incredible chemistry and the crowd was mesmerized.

After performing a few more songs, Puff Daddy and Mase took a break to pay tribute to Notorious BIG. Puff Daddy recounted stories of his friendship with Biggie, and the crowd went silent out of respect.

That night was so special to me because it helped bonded me more with my father in a way that understood me. That concert I didn't need it to be with any of my friends my father was the coolest friend I could have ever asked for.

In elementary school, my classmates loved that I was already quite tall. This made me stand out and other kids were always curious about my height. They were fascinated and would often come up to me to ask questions or ask if I wanted to play. However, despite my height, I was a nerd with a big head and was more interested in books and learning than sports or other kids. I made friends with other kids who shared the same interests, and together we had fun exploring the world of books, math, and science. In Kindergarten, I was the tallest kid in class. The first day I met Branden and Steph, we had an instant connection. They were tall like me; it was like a tall kids club. As we got to know each other, we found out that we had a lot in common. We all enjoyed playing outside, exploring nature, and going on adventures. We were inseparable. For every sporting event, we were the first kids to be selected simply because we were tall; they automatically assumed if you're tall, you're athletic.

We shared so many special moments together, from running around the playground to attending each other's birthday parties and playing hide-and-seek. We used to love riding the bus together; we also called it the Cheese Wagon. We always teased each other and all the other kids in our class. We loved talking about video games. Each of us had an Atari and a Nintendo, and sometimes we would go over to each other's houses and play. There was that one time our parents got us a Game Boy and a Game Gear. I brought my Game Boy to school, and we all took turns playing it in the lunchroom. Luckily, we didn't get in trouble.

School came easy for us, sometimes we got bored in class because the learning was so easy, and we were all very smart nerds. My parents always said, "You're growing up too fast, you're growing out of your clothes faster than we can buy them."

I loved being the tallest in my class at school. All the kids kind of gravitated towards me. Growing up in the 80s and 90s was a great time for my family. My mother and father were running their business, things were going extremely well, plus my father also worked in a lab as a scientist. My mom also had a side business running a small little daycare for people that she knew. My family used to give me the best Christmases. I used to have so many gifts and toys; I couldn't even play with them all, so we would donate them. They got me this big gold treasure chest to store all my toys in.

My love for books was truly special. I could spend hours getting lost in the pages and imagining the characters and their adventures. My favorite books were a mix of classic tales and modern adventures, each one offering a unique escape from the world around me.

One of my all-time favorites was "The Hobbit" by J.R.R. Tolkien. I was enthralled by the magical world of Middle-earth and the journey of the hobbit, Bilbo Baggins, as he embarked on a dangerous quest. I loved the themes of friendship, courage, and determination that were woven throughout the story.

Another one of my favorites was "Goosebumps" by R.L. Stine. I was captivated by the spooky stories and the suspenseful twists and turns that kept me on the edge of my seat. I also loved being scared, but also knowing that I was safe in the end.

Lastly, I loved Dr. Seuss's book "Green Eggs and Ham." The story of Sam-I-Am and his persistent efforts to convince the narrator to try the green eggs and ham made me laugh out loud every time I read the silly rhyming words and the hilarious storyline.

Being a kid in school was challenging for me, even though I was smart and always made the honor roll. My school didn't have much diversity, but it was easy for me to make friends. Branden and Steph never made me feel like an outsider and never saw me any differently. We played every sport we could in school football, basketball, baseball, kickball, and dodgeball. I was so big as a kid that they didn't allow me to play Little League football, which was kind of a bummer. They had a weight restriction, and I was above it. I definitely wanted to play with my friends. My friends and I also loved playing video games. We had every gaming console you could think of, from Nintendo, Super Nintendo, and PlayStation.

We would have tournaments on the weekends, and the loser would have to buy pizza for everyone. I wasn't the most coordinated kid when it came to sports. Being tall, they automatically nominated me to play center in basketball, and I'd score all the points in the paint. My father would just say, "You're just a mini little Kareem."

But despite my lack of coordination, I was determined to improve. I would spend hours practicing my shots and footwork, studying videos of the greats like Kareem and Shaq. I was lucky to have a coach who believed in me and pushed me to be better every day. He would run drills with me after practice, and I would stay late to put up extra shots. All that hard work paid off, and by the time I was in high school, I was one of the top players on the team. I still wasn't the most graceful athlete on the court, but I was a force to be reckoned with in the paint. I could block shots, grab rebounds, and score with ease. Most importantly, I was having fun. I had a love for the game that was unrivaled, and I felt like I was doing something special every time I stepped onto the court.

The year 1996 was a pivotal time in my childhood. I saw a seismic shift within my family, and the experience impacted me deeply. In March, my aunt and my grandfather got sick. I remember the night vividly. I was upstairs in my room, and the rest of the bedrooms were downstairs. That night, I looked out of my bedroom window, and I saw an ambulance driving away. It turned out it was my aunt who had gotten extremely sick. My family didn't want to scare me, so they just left me in my room. The next day, I was at school, and my family went to the hospital to visit my aunt, where she was admitted. At the hospital, my grandfather collapsed in the elevator, and they had to admit him to the emergency room.

My father picked me up from school that day and told me that we had to go over to the hospital because my grandfather and my aunt were not doing so well. It was scary in my mind, but it was the first time I experienced a sense of sadness. When we arrived, my aunt had just finished having surgery for a heart problem. Meanwhile, my grandfather was diagnosed with pneumonia. I was sitting in his room with my father, and the nurse came into my grandfather's room. I remember she was checking his vitals and holding his wrist for a long time, and she had a puzzled look on her face. She looked over at my father and told him that he wasn't going to make it. In that very moment, I sat there and watched my grandfather peacefully transition, and his last words were he called my name. I'm not sure if he was trying to get my attention or my father's since we have the same name. My father was perplexed because he didn't know how he was going to break the news to my mother that her father was not going to make it. At that moment, I knew I was going to have to be strong for my grandmother and my mom. I didn't want to think about what I was feeling, but when I saw my mom and grandmother walking back into the hospital room, and my father delivers the news, it hit me hard. This was the first time I witnessed immense sadness in my family. Seeing my grandmother cry for the first time was very surreal. Knowing that this was the man that she had spent 56 years of her life with, and he was no longer here, the man that I admired, that was so strong, that could do so many things, it was literally like watching the loss of Superman. In the days and weeks that followed, I struggled to come to terms with what had happened. My family leaned on each other for support, and we mourned together. Despite the sadness, I also felt a sense of gratitude for the time I had with my grandfather. He had been a constant presence in my life, and I had so many fond memories of him. His passing taught me the importance of cherishing the people we love while they're still with us.

Over time, I learned to cope with the loss, but it left a lasting impact on me. It made me realize how precious life is and how important it is to make the most of the time we have. It also made me appreciate my family and friends even more, and I vowed to never take them for granted. I still think about my grandfather often, and I feel a sense of pride knowing that he played a role in shaping the person I am today.

After my grandfather's passing, my family grew stronger. My aunt's health never fully recovered, so my mom became her caretaker at home. Witnessing my mom take care of the family and being the strong matriarch that she is, I looked at her like she was Wonder Woman. It was during this moment that I wanted to be strong, just like my grandfather, father, and mother. But not only did I have the fascination and intrigue of being that way psychologically, but I also wanted to be that way physiologically. I used to love watching Arnold Schwarzenegger movies, and it inspired me to be big and strong like that.

In August of 1996, as I was transitioning into getting ready for high school, my father took me to the gym, and he wanted to teach me something early that he had learned late. He told me, "I want you to take care of your body and your health. Without good health, you really can't enjoy life to the fullest."

He was right, and I kept that motto in the back of my mind as I started to learn about health and fitness. Physical Education and History were my favorite subjects. After school, I would go to the school gym and learn to master the art of Exercise Science and Kinesiology. My friends and coaches definitely saw my results, and they were trying to recruit me to play football, but I just didn't have the interest. I loved being competitive in the gym. In high school, I was this tall, big gym jock that was a complete nerd. It was like looking at the Hulk with glasses on, but I loved it. I didn't have any bullies, and I spent a lot of time in the library, always reading fascinated with books and computers. I loved computers, and that became another fascination. My father and I went to RadioShack, and he bought me my first computer, a Packard Bell with Windows 95.

After taking such pride in my health, I did experience my fair share of visiting the doctor. I just had bad luck at times playing random sports. First, I sprained my neck after playing a pick-up game of soccer, and I was in the hospital for over a week. Second, I broke my nose playing basketball with my friends and family. Third, I was in the hospital for a week with pneumonia, and that was a scary moment. My temperature was high, and I started having seizures. Each one of these experiences made me resilient.

I learned that life can be unpredictable, and even if we take care of ourselves, accidents and illnesses can still happen. However, I didn't let these setbacks stop me from pursuing my interests and passions. I continued to prioritize my health and fitness, and I found joy in reading and learning about new things.

As I got older, I realized that taking care of my health wasn't just about being physically strong, but also mentally and emotionally strong. I faced challenges and difficult situations, but I learned to cope and overcome them with resilience and a positive mindset. I also recognized the importance of seeking help and support from others when I needed it.

I am grateful for the lessons that my experiences taught me. They shaped me into the person I am today and prepared me for the challenges and opportunities that lay ahead. I am proud of the person I have become, and I continue to prioritize my health and well-being while pursuing my interests and goals.

## High School

High school led me to a new world, not just with computers and technology, but also by expanding my social circle. I was starting to gain a lot of attention, and my mother pulled me aside to teach me about the birds and the bees, reminding me that I was not ready to be a grandmother. In that moment, I knew my focus had to be keeping my grades up and staying focused, although I did have my moments of talking to girls as I went through the cycle of adolescence.

During recess, I was walking with my friends out of class when I saw a new student who had transferred in. It was my very first high school crush, Sasha. She was tall, about 5'10", with beautiful caramel skin, long black hair, beautiful lips, and a smile that could brighten the darkest moment. She was Photoshop perfect, and all the guys in the school wanted to be with her. I remember the first time she walked past me; the scent of her perfume radiated throughout the entire hallway, and she smelled amazing. I couldn't help but ogle and navel-gaze at what it would be like to be with her.

I even dreamed about her; I was smitten, and it was a challenge to even talk to her. I was determined, so I joined the debate team just so I could see her at the competitions. She was in the drama club, and I would always show up to their plays, even though I wasn't a big fan of the arts. I mustered up the courage to talk to her after one of their shows, and I was shocked that she was nice and easy to talk to. From that moment, we instantly bonded, hanging out more and more. We would grab lunch together, go to the movies, and just walk around the park talking about life. It was during this time that I realized I was falling in love with her. I remember the day I mustered up the courage to tell her how I felt; I was so nervous, but it was the best decision I ever made. She felt the same way, and we started dating. It was the best time of my life; she was my first love, and it was so pure and innocent. But when I woke up the next morning, I realized it was all a dream, and I was so disappointed.

I felt she was so far out of my league, and I lacked self-confidence to shoot my shot. I never worked up the confidence to introduce myself to her. That was definitely one of those moments where I could have used some liquid courage, but I was never a drinker. I started to develop more of a social consciousness around the type of woman I'm attracted to and who I could see myself with.

One day after school, my father told me we were going to the DMV to get my learner's permit and learn how to drive. This was a perfect opportunity for him because now I became his chauffeur. My father had me driving everywhere; I had so much practice that by the time I got my official driver's license, I believed I had put in more hours than what you need to get a pilot license. As I got older and started to drive more, I learned to appreciate the freedom that came with it. I loved being able to go wherever I wanted and explore unfamiliar places. My father and I would take long drives just to see where the road would take us, and we always had a great time. He would tell me stories about his travels when he was younger and share all the lessons he had learned throughout his life. These drives and conversations with my father instilled in me a sense of adventure and curiosity about the world. I learned to embrace the journey and always be open to new experiences.

## Meeting Distant Family

I grew up mostly around my mom's family, so when my father mentioned that he was going to introduce me to some of his family, I was intrigued. We took many road trips during the summer months, and he had me drive to Columbus, OH, to see my aunts. It was also during this time that I got to meet my three half-brothers and my half-sister from my father's previous marriage. The idea of meeting them was so fascinating to me, even though we were far apart. Knowing that I had distant siblings made me wonder what it could have been like if we were close. They were so much older than me, living their own lives, and I didn't really get a chance to spend much time with them. It was during that moment that I realized there were a lot of tall, big people on my father's side of the family. Now I understand where I get my size from.

I was excited to finally meet my half-siblings and see what kind of people they were. They were all very welcoming, and it was great to get to know them a little bit. My father's side of the family was full of big personalities, and it was so much fun to be around them. I was always the tallest kid in my class, but seeing how tall my half-siblings were made me feel like I wasn't so unique after all. I remember my father telling me stories about how tall his family was and how many were great athletes. I felt proud to be part of such a tall and athletic family. It turns out we had a few former NFL players in the family.

After spending some time with my half-siblings, I realized that we had a lot in common despite the vast age difference. They were a lot older than I, but we all loved sports, music, and movies. We would spend hours talking about our favorite teams and players. I was happy to have finally found some people who shared my interests. We continued to keep in touch even after our road trip was over, and I felt lucky to have them as part of my life.

That road trip with my father and meeting my half-siblings was a great experience that I would never forget. It was a time in my life when I learned about the importance of family and how it can shape who you are. I was grateful for the opportunity to meet my half-siblings and learn about my family's history and traditions.


My First Car


One day after school, my father surprised me again and took me to the dealership to look at cars. In the back of my mind, I thought he wanted me to help him look for a new car since he was always a car guy. He showed me pictures of himself when he was younger and had bought a powder blue convertible Cadillac Coupe

Deville. I knew that whatever car my father was going to purchase, it was going to be of very classy and regal taste. When we arrived at the dealership, he drove to the back, and we pulled up to a beautiful royal blue four-door Infiniti with gold trim. It was magnificent, truly a show-stopper of a car. I told my father, "You and mom are going to look great in this car. She's going to love this."

My father then said to me, "This is not for me and your mom. This is your first car."

I was completely baffled, excited, overjoyed, and jubilant; it was such a surreal moment. My father told me that my mother and he were extremely proud of me, that I had always been a good kid and never given them any trouble. He then mentioned the conditions with the car: I could not be out past eleven at night, and if I were late, I had to call them ahead of time. That was the curfew, and I had to check with them every two hours. I followed my father in my new car all the way home. I loved how it handled on the road, and the sound system was amazing. When we got home, my mother was absolutely shocked at what my father had just done. He explained to her why he did it, and she happily agreed. The next day, I drove it to my high school, and all my friends loved it. They were asking me if I could give them a ride. After school, we used to go to a place down the street that we called "the slab." It was our community basketball court. One of my friends said to me, "Max, roll down the windows and put some music on. I left my CDs at home."

So I put on an album called The Score by The Fugees. It sounded amazing in my car; the Bose sound system was unbelievable. It sounded like a concert was happening by the basketball court. During this time, I felt like the coolest kid in school. We played basketball for a little bit, and then I got hungry and wanted to head home to get some of my mom's food.

## My First Speeding Ticket

After leaving school, I wanted to take a drive into town; I wasn't ready to go home just yet. The next thing I heard were police sirens, and I got so nervous. Then I realized the cop was pulling me over. Waiting with anticipation for him to walk up to my car, I started sweating from nervousness. The policeman walked up slowly to my car, and I rolled the window down. He asked for my license and registration, so I handed him my license, and then I reached into the glove compartment for the registration. He took a brief glance at both and then asked me the weirdest question I never thought a policeman would ask. He asked me, "Is this your car?"

I paused for a second and said, "Yes, sir, it is."

In the back of my mind, I started to feel sorry for him; I was pulled over by a police officer who was completely illiterate. He couldn't read that my name was on my license and registration. Actually, the registration was in my father's name, but since we have the same name, you get the point. Then he proceeded to ask me, "Do you know why I pulled you over?"

I said to him, "Sir, I'm sorry, but I don't. I was just cruising."

He said, "I clocked you doing 42 in a 25."

I said to the officer, "I saw the speed limit say 35."

And he said, "It changes to 25 once you get past the baseball field."

I immediately apologized and told him I did not see that sign. Then he proceeded to walk back to his car and write up the ticket. I was so scared that I was going to get grounded. I didn't want my parents thinking I'm out here speeding and acting crazy behind the wheel. He handed me the ticket and told me that I was three miles away from being charged with reckless driving. The officer ended up only writing me a ticket for 42 in a 35. That was a huge sigh of relief because I'm sure that ticket would have had a much higher fine to pay.

When I arrived home, I was still nervous to tell my parents. My father hadn't arrived home yet, so I immediately went and talked to my mom about it. Moms always know when something is wrong, and my mom knew it was written all over my face. I told my mom I got a speeding ticket, and she said, "Let me see it."

It seems like he wrote you a ticket for going 7 miles over the speed limit. I didn't want to lie, so I told my mum the whole story. My mom looked at me and said, "Don't worry about it; I'll take care of it."

She said to me, "I appreciate your integrity. You are not in trouble."

I felt a huge sigh of relief in my mind. I thought I was going to be grounded, the car would be confiscated; I was just thinking about every worst-case scenario possible.

A few hours later, my father arrived, and my mom told him that I got my first speeding ticket. She showed him the ticket while we were all eating dinner. My father said, "Who writes a ticket for seven miles over the speed limit?"

Then I had to tell my father the whole transparent story. My father responded and said, "I believe we can go to court and get this thrown out so it doesn't count against your record."

The whole time, I thought they were going to ground me. Instead, they were coming up with a solution of how to get out of this ticket. I believe my parents knew there was more to the story, but they were testing me to see if I was going to be honest.

The valuable lesson I learned that day is when you're honest and transparent things work out better on your behalf then when you try to lie and cover it up. My father and I went to court, and the ticket was dismissed. I learned a valuable lesson that day about honesty and the importance of owning up to my mistakes. It was a wake-up call that reminded me that driving is a serious responsibility, and I needed to be more careful on the road.

## Columbine

After school one day, I came home to an unusually quiet house. I could sense that something was wrong. As I entered the living room, I saw my family gathered around the television, and their faces were filled with shock and disbelief. The news was reporting on a school shooting in Littleton, Colorado, and as I watched the footage of children running for their lives, I felt an overwhelming sadness and despair. It was a tragedy that I never thought could happen at a school, and it made me realize that my own safety could be compromised at any moment. I looked at my mother, who was in tears. She is the most empathetic person I know, and I could tell that she was not only thinking about the children who were affected, but also the mothers who had lost their children. We hugged each other tightly and told each other how much we loved each other. That night, my family gathered in the living room and prayed for all those involved. It was a somber moment that left a lasting impact on all of us.

The events in Littleton had a profound impact on me. It made me realize how fragile life is and how easily it can be taken away. I started to appreciate my family and friends more, and I made a conscious effort to let them know how much I love and care about them. It also made me appreciate the safety and security of my school even more. I started to pay closer attention to the safety drills we had and took them more seriously.

Bonding with my Uncle

Shortly after school let out for the summer, my mom told me that I was going to stay with my uncle, who lived in the suburban town of Fredericksburg, VA, just south of Washington DC. I had always admired my uncle, who was a very successful bourgeois working for the US government. This was a great opportunity for me to bond with him and stay at his home for a week. I was very curious and mystified about what my uncle was going to show me and what we were going to do.

I was excited about the road trip to his house. When we arrived, I loved the neighborhood. There were so many different kids playing in the yard. It was nothing like where I lived. Once we pulled into the driveway, my uncle greeted us.

The house was located in a peaceful and serene neighborhood, surrounded by lush green trees. As you approached the house, you were immediately struck by its charming facade. The home was painted a warm and inviting shade of yellow, with white trim around the windows and doors. A sprawling porch wrapped around the front of the house, complete with rocking chairs and potted plants.

Stepping inside, we were greeted by a grand foyer with a gleaming hardwood floor. To the left was a cozy sitting room with plush sofas and armchairs, and to the right was a formal dining room with a mahogany table and China cabinet. Beyond the foyer was the heart of the home, a spacious and bright living room with a fireplace and large windows overlooking the backyard.

Upstairs, there were four bedrooms, each one more beautiful than the last. The master suite was a true oasis, with a king-sized bed, a spa-like bathroom, and a private balcony with breathtaking views of the surrounding neighborhood. The other bedrooms were also well-appointed, each one with its own unique style and character.

The backyard of the home was a true paradise, with a charming gazebo and a well-manicured lawn. After he gave us the grand tour, I said to myself, "This is the kind of home I could see myself living in."

I was instantly inspired. My uncle was an extremely hard worker who didn't talk much about what he did.

He just allowed his success to make all the noise, and he was very humble about it, which I admired.

He's also an amazing cook. I watched him make his signature dish, Candied Yams. It wasn't even Thanksgiving, and he made some just for me. I was mesmerized as my stomach growled, watching as he peeled and sliced the yams into rounds or wedges, then arranged them in a baking dish. He applied a candied syrup made by melting butter in a saucepan, adding brown sugar and spices, and then stirring in a splash of orange juice or maple syrup for added depth of flavor. This syrup was then poured over the yams in the baking dish, ensuring that each slice was well coated.

The yams were then baked in the oven until they were tender and golden brown. The warm syrup created a glaze on the yams that was sticky, sweet, and delicious. The yams could be served as a side dish or as a dessert, topped with a scoop of vanilla ice cream and a sprinkle of chopped pecans.

When I heard the bell go off in the kitchen that the yams were ready, I immediately rushed to the dining room table, anxious and ready for dinner the first night. Dinner was exceptional that night. I went back for seconds, and then I had another plate.

As I got to know my uncle, I realized that he and I shared a fascination for technology. We would talk about programming, networking, databases, and all the latest technology. I found out what he did for a living and was instantly inspired. Now I see why my mom wanted me to spend time with him because she saw similarities between us.

I would often go to him for advice on the latest gadgets and trends, and he was always more than happy to oblige. He had an impressive knowledge of the field and would share stories of his time as a professional in the industry.

I remember one of his stories that particularly stood out to me. He had worked on a project to create a new system that would revolutionize the way people interacted at his workplace. He told me about the trials and tribulations he encountered while developing this system and how the team he was working with was extremely passionate about their work. They eventually created a product that was both innovative and efficient, and it was sent for production to be accessible to people all over the organization.

The next day, he took me on a tour of his workplace and showed me his office. I was so inspired that I felt like a big kid in a candy store around all this technology. I looked at him like I was around Steve Jobs. That was the moment when I knew that this was what I wanted to do; I wanted to be like him.

At the end of that week, on my way home, I thought about my future and what it would take to get to that level and be like my uncle. I wanted to be a part of greatness and excellence, just like him.

## My First Job

During the summers, I always wanted to figure out ways to make money, so I tried working in fast food, but I didn't like coming home smelling like food all the time. I also worked as a bagger in the grocery store, which I loved because I always got to meet people.

Then, my parents granted me the opportunity to work with the family in their landscaping and janitorial business after school. This allowed me to see firsthand the hard work and dedication it took to run a successful operation. My parents were always busy, whether it was meeting with clients, managing finances, or overseeing the day-to-day operations.

Despite the long hours and stressful situations, my parents never wavered in their commitment to the business. They showed me the importance of setting goals, working efficiently, and most importantly, never giving up. They taught me that success in business and life comes from hard work and determination.

I learned about the value of teamwork and communication. I saw how everyone had to come together and do their part for the business to thrive. These lessons have stayed with me throughout my life and have helped shape my approach to work and leadership.

One time, when I came to work with my parents, my mom asked me to help organize the office and put away some extra supplies. To my surprise, my father had hidden a box of donuts behind some boxes of paper on the top shelf. I was so excited to find them that I immediately started devouring them!

My mom was not impressed. She scolded me for eating all the donuts and not helping out with the work she had asked me to do. My father, on the other hand, was laughing so hard that he had tears streaming down his face.

Needless to say, I was allowed to finish the donuts on the condition that I would finish the rest of the work afterward.

# Fixing the Cars

My father always had so many cars in the driveway, including antiques and new cars, and I loved it. He was trying to teach me the art of how to work on cars, and it certainly fascinated me to learn how a combustible engine works. My father taught me that in life, you need to learn how to do things for yourself, as self-sufficiency and self-education are key as an adult. So he began teaching me all the intricacies of fixing cars and their parts. My father and I were both tall, big men, so it was often challenging with our large hands to fix certain things in small, tight spaces. Nevertheless, I loved that this was another moment where we were building quality time together.

One day, my father decided to show me how to change the spark plugs. He handed me the socket wrench and asked me to loosen the first spark plug. I put all my strength into it, but instead of loosening the spark plug, I ended up rounding the hex head. My father couldn't stop laughing as he shook his head and told me, "Well, that's a rookie mistake."

Another time, we were working on the engine and trying to tighten a bolt. My father instructed me to hold the wrench steady, but as he tightened the bolt, the wrench slipped out of my hand and hit him squarely in the face. The two of us were laughing so hard that it took a few minutes for my father to regain his composure.

Although there were some funny mishaps along the way, my father's lessons on working on the pickup truck taught me valuable skills and instilled in me a love for all things mechanical.

My father and I continued to work on cars together throughout my teenage years. As I grew more confident in my abilities, I would often take on more complicated projects with his guidance. I enjoyed the challenge of diagnosing problems and finding solutions. I realize how fortunate I was to have a father who was willing to teach me such valuable skills. Not only did he teach me about cars, but he also taught me about the importance of hard work, perseverance, and self-sufficiency.

# Chapter 3

It was the last year of high school, and the dot-com era was at its peak. We were also experiencing our very first energy crisis, as gas prices started to rise for the first time. I used to be able to go anywhere I wanted to go with just ten dollars of gas in my car. Another turning point in my teenage life, my senior year of high school, was supposed to be focused on getting ready for college and trying to decide where I wanted to go. However, my family experienced another catastrophe that changed everything.

One morning, I was in my room getting ready for school when my mom came running to my door and urgently told me to get up. I rushed downstairs and walked into my parents' room to find my father laying on the floor, unable to get up. In that moment, I had to be strong for my mom because my father had just had a stroke. I lifted up the strongest man I knew off the ground because he could not lift himself. It was a life-altering moment for me. As a teenager, I had to step up and be the man of the house. My father was always the one who took care of us, but now it was my turn to help him. I was scared, but I knew I had to be strong for my family. I helped my mother take care of my father and made sure he got the best medical care possible. It was a challenging time, but we made it through together as a family. The experience taught me the importance of taking care of those you love and being there for them in their time of need. From that day on, I made a promise to always be there for my family and to always put them first.

That day changed the course of our family forever. My father, the protector, provider, and the most hardworking individual I know, was never the same, even after he went through all the rehab to try to get back to being 100%. He just couldn't work like he used to. My mother had to become Wonder Woman, taking care of my father, my aunt, and my grandmother who was experiencing early signs of Alzheimer's.

We visited him every day in the hospital, bringing him whatever he needed to make him comfortable. It was tough seeing him struggle, but we all knew that he was a fighter and would pull through. After months of therapy and rehabilitation, my father finally came home. He still had a long road ahead of him, but we were all there to support him every step of the way.

I learned so much from this experience. It taught me the importance of the power of love, faith, and support during difficult times. I witnessed my mother pick up the mantle and be strong for the entire family. Her herculean effort showed the selflessness and love that she has for the family, which instilled in me the importance of having that kind of love from my future family.

Witnessing my father become extremely depressed because of his condition, a true alpha male who could not take care of himself and be independent, I had to do what I could to support my mom in any way I could. That meant putting off college because I was afraid to leave.

From that moment on, I knew I wanted to be like my mother to have her strength and selflessness in taking care of the people I love. I also learned the importance of taking care of my own health and well-being, so I wouldn't end up like my father. I started making healthier choices, eating right, and exercising regularly. I also paid more attention to my mental health and sought support when I needed it.

My father's health slowly improved over time, and he eventually regained the ability to walk, although he never fully regained all his strength. He always reminded me of how proud he was of me and my mother.

During this time, I was dating someone named Tonya. She lived in the next county over from me, and we had grown very close. Our families knew each other, and we sometimes went to church together, even though we went to different churches. She was a beautiful soul. On one Sunday afternoon, I received devastating news – she had died in a car wreck right after leaving church. I was in a very dark state during this period, with everything that was going on with my family and now this loss.

Losing someone you love and care about deeply is never easy, and I remember feeling lost and confused, trying to understand why this had happened. I struggled to come to terms with her passing, and it felt like everything around me was falling apart.

But despite all of that, I still had my family to lean on. They were my support system, and they helped me get through this difficult time. I also found solace in my faith and the idea that Tonya was now in a better place, free from all the pain and suffering of this world.

Virginia Tech Football

I wanted to plan something special for my family. My mother and father needed a moment to escape from so much that was going on. So, I decided that we should all go to a Virginia Tech game during the time when Michael Vick was the most popular athlete in the state of Virginia. My parents became huge fans of watching him play. Virginia Tech was having an unbelievable season on their run to the national championship.

We went over and watched a game, and we had a phenomenal time. It was just what we needed. The stadium was huge and filled with people, making it all the more exciting. As the game started, my parents and I watched in awe as Michael Vick took charge of the offense. His passes were accurate, and the way he maneuvered was electric. It was clear that he was a prodigy who knew the game of football inside and out.

Watching my mom shout and cheer along with my father, I was more excited and thrilled to see them be happy than to watch the game, even though it was a good game. Plus, we had a chance to be part of history.


College Prep


To be there for my mother, I put off moving out and going to college, but I enrolled myself in community college after I graduated high school. I wasn't as happy as I wanted to be, but I knew I had to put my own interests aside and support my family. One day, I came home from school and observed my mother in the kitchen, preparing meals for everyone. I was fascinated by how she had the energy to be a caretaker and make time for herself.

It was sad for me at times watching my aunt bedridden, my grandmother not as cognitively coherent as she used to be, and my father struggling to walk. I hated that I had to see the quality of life that was just not there for my family any longer. I became immensely sad and very depressed, and one day my mother pulled me aside. She automatically knew what was wrong with me without me having to say anything. We both had to comfort each other in a way we thought we never had to. She told me, "I don't want you to stay here. I want you to go live your life. This is not your cross to bear."

She was right. I didn't want to stay, but I was ready to start a new transition in my life. I sat down in my room and began making plans for a transition to where I saw myself in the next few years. Then the idea hit me: I want to go live in Washington, DC. I already had family there, it was close enough if I needed to come home, but far away enough so I could really experience and explore the urban metropolitan life. She told me that she wanted me to follow my dreams, pursue my degree.

It was then that I realized that being there for my family didn't mean staying by their side all the time, but rather being able to support them from a distance. I transferred to a four-year university and started on my path toward my future. I will never forget the love and sacrifices that my mother made for our family, and I will always be grateful for her guidance and wisdom.

It was a Friday night, and my friends from the community college invited me out to a party at Virginia Tech. I was never really a big party type of kid, but I accepted the invitation. It was a perfect time to just get my mind off things with everything going on. The party was hosted at the Sheraton Hotel Ballroom, which was very cool. However, I'm not good at being social at parties, so I found myself leaning against the wall just observing the crowd.

Then, there was this one girl who was looking at me. She was very attractive, about 5'9 with short black hair and a very sexy, glass coke bottle body. She walked over to me and told me, "You seem like you're not having a good time."

I smiled and said, "I am, I'm just taking it all in. This is the first college party I've ever been to."

So I introduced myself, and she said, "I'm Natalie."

We started dancing together, and she said, "I love this song."

In the back of my mind, I knew I had no rhythm, but she knew how to loosen me up. After dancing for a while, she started telling me a little about herself and asked if I went to Virginia Tech. I replied, "No, I don't. I'm going to the community college because I just graduated high school."

She then told me, "I go to Radford University, and I'm on the track team."

She grabbed me by my hands and wrapped them around her body, and at that moment, it was exactly what I needed to get my mind off everything. She could tell I was getting more relaxed and comfortable with her, so we danced for the rest of the night together. At the end of the night, she gave me her phone number.

Natalie and I had hit it off quickly, we decided to go on a few dates to get to know each other better. On the first date, we went out to dinner at one of our favorite restaurants. We talked for hours, getting to know each other's interests, dreams, and aspirations. We laughed, teased each other, and generally had a great time.

On our second date, we decided to take a romantic walk in the park. As we strolled around, we held hands and caught up on the events of the week. We talked about our families and plans for the future. Natalie mentioned that she was interested in transitioning to Florida after college, and I told her that I was also planning to transition myself. We watched the sunset and the stars come out, savoring the peaceful moment.

Finally, on our last date, we went to a movie. We cuddled up in the theater, watching the movie and enjoying the moment together. It was the perfect way to end our brief but beautiful courtship. Sadly, soon after, Natalie had to leave town and we said our goodbyes. Although brief, our time together was filled with special memories.

Weeks went by as I planned my transition. I wanted to experience more diversity, not only in culture but also in thought. I wanted to explore different norms and values than the ones I had grown up with, and to challenge myself to break out of my comfort zone. With the support and encouragement of my mother, I packed up and headed out to start a new chapter in my life.

At first, I knew it would be difficult to adjust to a new environment and meet people, but I remained confident. I wanted to find a new group of friends from different backgrounds who had unique perspectives. I aimed to explore different clubs and organizations and to get involved in activities that I was passionate about. Gradually, I found my voice and place in the world. Despite the hardships and challenges I faced, I grew so much and became a stronger, more resilient person. I was grateful for the experiences and memories I had made and I knew that I was on the right path to becoming the person I wanted to be.

# Chapter 4

In the summer of 2001, I was excited to take my first trip with my father to Washington DC, passing through the beautiful scenic side of Virginia and seeing Shenandoah. Once we arrived, we stopped at my aunt's house in Lorton, VA. She and my uncle had been living in the Washington area for a long time. This was also my first time driving in the city, and I just loved every aspect of what I was experiencing. Washington DC at that time had so many prolific scholars and still does, like Bill Nye the Science Guy, Dr. Michael Eric Dyson, and even General Colin Powell. I knew that as soon as I stepped on the soil of the National Mall, this is exactly where I wanted to be. I wanted to make my mark.

As the days went on, my father and I explored the city, visiting all the monuments, museums, and historical landmarks that Washington DC had to offer. I was in awe of all the history that surrounded me, from the Lincoln Memorial to the Thomas Jefferson Memorial. I was also inspired by all the people who had made such a big impact on the world and had their names etched in stone for all to see.

We also had the chance to attend a lecture at the National Museum of American History, where I heard a renowned historian speak about the Civil Rights Movement. That was an experience that I will never forget. It was amazing to see how a movement that started with a few brave people, who stood up for their rights, eventually led to a country-wide movement that changed the course of history.

That trip to Washington DC was a life-changing experience for me. It opened my eyes to a world of possibilities and made me realize that I too could make a difference in the world.

The next day, we went to the National Mall to visit the Lincoln Memorial and the Washington Monument. I was awestruck by the size and grandeur of these monuments, and I was so inspired by the stories of these great leaders. I also had the opportunity to visit the Smithsonian Museums, which were filled with history and knowledge. I learned so much about different cultures and the history of our country.

That trip to Washington DC changed me, and I knew that I wanted to be a part of the positive change that was happening in the world. I returned to the hotel with a renewed sense of purpose, and I wanted to become more involved in community service and advocacy work. I thought about changing my major to Political Science, and I focused on studying the policies and systems that affect people's lives. I felt that I had a greater understanding of the world and my place in it, and I was determined to use my education and experience to make a positive impact.

We continued our tour and drove through Dupont Circle, where we saw people hanging out and enjoying the nightlife. As we drove through the historic streets of DC, we couldn't help but admire the stunning architecture of the buildings, especially the National

Cathedral. We also passed by the Lincoln Memorial, where people were taking pictures and enjoying the peaceful surroundings.

Reaching the National Mall, the sight of the Washington Monument lit up in the night sky was breathtaking. We saw the Lincoln Memorial Reflecting Pool, where we admired the reflection of the Lincoln Memorial in the calm waters.

The tour was unforgettable. It was a clear, chilly evening and the city lights illuminated the dark sky. My cousin was an excellent tour guide, showing us all the best spots in downtown DC. We first stopped at DC Live, where we enjoyed a live performance by a local band. The atmosphere was electric, and the music was fantastic. From there, we drove to Coco Loco, a unique bar and restaurant that served some of the best Latin-inspired cocktails and cuisine.

Next, we explored Georgetown, which was one of my favorite parts of the tour. The cobblestone streets added to the charm and character of the area, and we loved seeing all the historic buildings and quaint shops. From Georgetown, we drove down to Foggy Bottom and Pennsylvania Ave, catching a glimpse of the White House in the distance.

Finally, we drove down Connecticut Ave and stopped at 1223, a trendy bar and lounge that was packed with people. Across the street was 18th Street Lounge, known for its live jazz music and cozy atmosphere. We ended up spending the rest of the night there, listening to some of the best jazz musicians in the city.

Overall, it was a memorable night filled with new experiences and lots of fun. I was grateful to have a cousin who knew the city so well and was willing to show us around.

After the tour, we headed to one of the most iconic food spots in DC: Ben's Chili Bowl. The place was buzzing with activity, and the aroma of delicious food wafted through the air. I was excited to try their famous chili dogs and smothered fries, and I wasn't disappointed. The taste of the juicy hot dogs and the spicy chili sauce was simply amazing, and I'll never forget my first bite.

Next, we tried the Mambo sauce, which was a new experience for me. The sweet and tangy sauce added an extra burst of flavor to our food, and I was hooked. I remember trying to find a bottle to take home with me, but unfortunately, no luck there.

Overall, the night tour of DC was a truly unforgettable experience, and I was grateful for the opportunity to try new food and learn about different cultures. I can't wait to go back and explore more of what the city has to offer. I returned home with a newfound sense of purpose and determination to follow my dreams, no matter how big or small they might seem.

Moving and transitioning to DMV

I decided to stay with my family in Maryland until I got my bearings. It's amazing how another name for Washington DC is the DMV which means DC, Maryland, and Virginia. There is a completely different culture in Maryland than there is in Northern Virginia, and I was fascinated by the differences.

My first job was part-time at the Social Security Administration (SSA) which allowed me to meet new people and gain valuable work experience. I worked with a diverse group of individuals, and I was able to learn about their backgrounds and cultures, which added to my appreciation of the DMV area.

In my free time, I explored Northern Virginia and DC even more. I visited other museums, art galleries, and historical sites that I didn't see when I first toured DC with my father and cousin. I also attended local events and festivals, where I got to try new foods and listen to live music.

As I continued my studies, I also took advantage of the opportunity to intern at a few different organizations in the DMV area. These internships provided me with hands-on experience in my field of study, and I was able to network with professionals in the industry. The SSA office had an amazing view, as it was in the tallest building in Northern Virginia, and I could see the entire landscape of Northern Virginia and DC.

## 9/11

I was scheduled to work because I didn't have a class that morning. Within the first 25 minutes of being there, our office received a phone call that the Pentagon had just been bombed. The paralegal who answered the phone was incredibly shocked. This was the day of 9/11 that will live in infamy. We immediately packed up and headed out of the building because we were concerned that a plane was going to hit our building. It was an incredibly scary moment for me because at the time, my uncle worked at the

Department of Defense. We all thought his office was still in the Pentagon, but we couldn't reach him. It was mass chaos all over the DMV area. They had shut down the metro, so everyone had to find a ride home. Luckily, I drove to work that day, but traffic was pandemonium, and it took me forever to get home.

Once I finally arrived home, I turned on the news to try and find out more information. The images of the towers collapsing, and the Pentagon burning were surreal, and I was filled with a mixture of shock, fear, and sadness.

For the rest of the day, my family and I tried to reach my uncle, but all the phone lines were jammed. We were all in a state of panic, not knowing if he was safe or not. It wasn't until later that night that we finally heard from him, and he was thankfully safe. So many other families were not as fortunate.

The events of 9/11 had a profound impact on me, and I will never forget that day. The bravery and selflessness of the first responders and the victims will always be remembered and honored. The DMV area and the country as a whole came together in the wake of the tragedy, and it was a powerful reminder of the strength and resilience of the American people.

In the days and weeks following 9/11, the DMV area was filled with a sense of unity and patriotism. People came together to support one another and honor those who lost their lives. Memorials and tributes were set up all over the area, and people visited them to pay their respects.

The attack on the Pentagon also brought about increased security measures and a heightened sense of awareness. The government increased its efforts to protect its citizens and prevent future attacks. In the DMV, there was a visible increase in security personnel and surveillance, and people were more cautious in their daily activities.

I also learned the importance of being grateful for each day and cherishing the time we have with our loved ones. The events of that day served as a reminder to never take our safety and security for granted and to always be vigilant in protecting our country.

The memory of 9/11 will always be with me, and I will always be proud of how the DMV area and the country as a whole came together in the face of tragedy. We will never forget the heroes who lost their lives and the bravery and resilience of the American people.

The experience of living in the DMV and being a part of the recovery after 9/11 only strengthened my resolve to further my education and make a difference in the world.

I realized that DMV was not just a city of politics and monuments but a city of diversity, culture, and opportunities. I made new friends from all over the world and learned about their cultures, experiences, and perspectives. This exposure to different cultures and ways of life broadened my horizons and taught me the importance of acceptance and empathy.

I also realized that DMV was not just a city of power but a city of resilience and strength. The people of DMV came together in the face of adversity and showed the world what it means to be truly united. This experience instilled in me a sense of pride in my country and a deep appreciation for the people who make it the great nation it is.

Today, I am proud to call DMV my home, and I am grateful for the experiences and lessons it has taught me. The city continues to inspire me every day, and I am honored to be a part of its rich history and vibrant community.

Being the first in my family to attend college, I knew I wanted to make them proud and was grateful for everything they had sacrificed for me. I was determined to make the most of this opportunity. I threw myself into my studies and soon found that I had a passion for technology and international relations. I was fascinated by the way different countries interacted with each other and how the decisions made in DMV had a profound impact on the entire world.

During my time at DMV, I also became involved in various community organizations, where I had the chance to give back to the city that had given me so much. I volunteered at local food banks, helped with disaster relief efforts, and even helped organize events to raise awareness for various social issues. Through these experiences, I discovered a deep sense of purpose and a desire to make a positive impact on the world.

One of my favorite volunteer experiences was working at a local food bank, where I was able to help distribute food and resources to families in need. Seeing homeless people for the first time was very moving for me. This experience taught me the importance of helping others and the impact that we can have on our community.

Living in the DMV empowered me to be smarter, to chase my goals, and to step outside of my circle and my comfort zone. At first, it was challenging, but what I've learned is if it doesn't challenge you, it doesn't change you. It changed me in ways I needed to be changed. It made me more self-aware culturally, politically, and educationally. It helped me break through the barriers of my naivete. I looked at Washington DC as the big brother I always needed. Being so engulfed and entrenched around so many educated people, just like my uncle, and listening to how they talked, their vernacular was so sophisticated that it was like I was learning another language in my own country.

The experience of volunteering to help pass the city ordinance was one of the most impactful experiences I had. I worked closely with community leaders and advocacy groups to educate residents and build support for the ordinance, which would improve the lives of low-income families. After months of hard work, the ordinance passed, and I was proud to have played a role in making a difference in the lives of those in need.

Washington DC was also a hub for cultural events and festivals. Every summer, the city came alive with the National Cherry Blossom Festival, and the streets were filled with visitors from all over the world. I also had the opportunity to attend concerts at the Kennedy Center, visit the Smithsonian museums, and enjoy the beautiful parks in the city.

The city had given me so much more than I could have ever imagined. It provided me with a wealth of experiences, opportunities, and friendships that I will cherish for a lifetime.

# Chapter 5

In college, I made friends of different cultures, which was a new and exciting experience for me. I had friends from Africa, Persia, Asia, and various parts of Europe. Listening to their stories about their cultures, norms, and values broadened my understanding of the world and taught me the importance of acceptance and diversity. I also made close friends who were veterans - one from the Navy, two from the Army, and one from the Marines. We are still friends to this day, and our bond is like that of brothers.

One of my Navy veteran friends, Calvin, was like an older brother to me. He knew I was from a small town, and he was from New Orleans, so he would often teach me about where he was from and what it was like growing up in New Orleans. The first time I went to his place, I was completely mystified. He had New Orleans Saints posters on the walls and Mardi Gras beads hanging on the cabinets. It was as if he had brought New Orleans to Washington DC. Calvin helped fill in the gaps of what I was missing, like teaching me how to talk to girls and the importance of living on my own. He introduced me to crawfish, and we even had a crawfish boil at his place, which was one of my favorite college memories.

These friendships and experiences taught me so much about myself and the world. They helped me become more self-aware and culturally competent, and I am grateful for the lasting impact they have had on my life.

Calvin was not just a friend, but also a mentor to me. He always had a smile on his face and a kind word to offer. He showed me that the world was big and diverse, and that there was so much to learn from other cultures. Despite coming from different backgrounds, he and I had an unbreakable bond.

One summer, Calvin invited me to join him in New Orleans. I was apprehensive at first, having never been to the Deep South before. However, Calvin made sure to show me all the best parts of the city and teach me about the rich culture and history of New Orleans. I was especially fascinated by the music scene, and Calvin took me to see some of the best jazz musicians in the city.

One day, we went to the famous Café du Monde for beignets and coffee. As we sat outside, sipping our coffee and watching the world go by, Calvin told me stories about his family and growing up in New Orleans. I was struck by how different his experiences were from mine, but at the same time, how much we had in common. He told me about the values he held dear and how important it was to be true to oneself.

I was so grateful for the time I spent with Calvin in New Orleans. Not only did I learn about a new city and its culture, but I also learned about myself. I came away from that summer with a new appreciation for the world and for the importance of relationships and connections. I will always be grateful for the friendship and guidance that Calvin provided, and I know that our bond will remain strong for many years to come.

My Army brother Peter grew up all over the world, but most of his family lives in North Carolina. I could easily relate to him because my family traveled to North Carolina a lot, especially to Greensboro and High Point. Another thing I found fascinating about him was his love for cars and being a big-time Carolina Panthers fan.

Growing up, Peter always had a love for cars. He was fascinated with the way they worked and the speed they could achieve. His love for cars eventually turned into a love for racing, and he began competing in local races.

As he got older, he joined the army and was stationed all over the world. Despite the constant changes, his love for cars never faded, and he always made sure to keep up with the latest models and trends.

One of his favorite things to do was visit his family in North Carolina, where they would all gather to watch the Carolina Panthers play on Sundays. Peter loved the energy and excitement that surrounded the games and was always eager to share his love for the sport with others.

Whenever he was back in North Carolina, he and his father would take trips to Greensboro and High Point, two cities that were famous for their car shows. They would spend hours looking at the different models and talking to the owners about their cars.

Despite the challenges that came with serving in the army, Peter never lost his love for cars and continued to chase his passion even while stationed overseas. To this day, he still watches the Carolina Panthers and participates in races whenever he can.

My second Army brother, Sampson, was from New Jersey, and I loved hanging out with him because he was a huge Philadelphia Eagles fan. He was a nerd like me in class, and we loved programming, so we had that in common.

Sampson and I quickly became close friends in college, bonding over our shared love of programming and our common appreciation for the Philadelphia Eagles, especially since my mom is a huge fan. Sampson would always tell me stories about growing up in New Jersey, from his family to the local culture. He was passionate about programming, and I loved listening to him talk about his latest projects and how he approached problem-solving in code.

One of my favorite memories with Sampson was when we decided to build a website together for a class project. It was a challenging project, but we were determined to make it a success. We spent hours working together in the library, trying out different coding techniques, and brainstorming new ideas. Our hard work paid off when we received an A on the project, and I was proud to have worked with such a talented and dedicated programmer like Sampson.

Aside from our shared interests in programming and football, I also appreciated Sampson's humor and quick wit. He was always cracking jokes and making us all laugh, and I felt lucky to have him as a friend.

My Air Force brother, Josh, was always the life of the party, like Calvin, always making sure that everyone was having a good time. He made the most delicious burgers and steaks you've ever tasted. Josh had a passion for good food, and he was always experimenting with new recipes and techniques.

Whenever we visited him, we knew we were in for a treat.

Despite being a huge Dallas Cowboys fan from Ohio, Josh was always the first to poke fun at himself. He loved to joke around, and we always had a good laugh at his expense. He never took things too seriously and was always the first to make a joke or lighten the mood.

One of the things that I loved about Josh was his dedication to his work in the Air Force. He was proud to serve his country and always talked about the places he had been and the experiences he had had. Despite the challenges he faced, he always had a positive attitude and was always quick to offer support and encouragement to his friends.

Overall, Josh was a great friend and an even better brother. He always put others first, and his kindness and generosity were unmatched. I will always cherish the memories I have of our times together and am grateful to have had him in my life.

My Marine brother Greg is from Seattle, and I absolutely loved hearing the marine stories he used to tell me. One day, I had the opportunity to meet his girlfriend, who was enrolled in dental school at Howard University. It was my first time meeting someone who was going to be in dental school, and I was fascinated by her dedication to helping others and the procedures she'd be performing one day.

One summer, Greg invited me to visit him in Seattle, and I was thrilled to see what life was like on the west coast. During my stay, Greg took me on a tour of the city, showing me all the best sights and sounds of the

Emerald City. We spent a day hiking in the mountains and fishing in Puget Sound, where I was fascinated by all the marine life in the water. I also asked Greg a million questions about his time in the Marines and loved hearing his stories.

But the highlight of my trip was spending time with Greg, his girlfriend, and their friends. At night, we would gather around the grill, where Greg would cook up a storm and tell us all about his adventures in the Marines. We would laugh and joke, sharing stories and making memories that would last a lifetime. When it was time to say goodbye, I felt a twinge of sadness, but I was grateful for the amazing time I had spent with my Marine brother and his friends. I knew that this was just the beginning of many great adventures to come.

One day, as I walked down to the student services building at school, I was pleasantly surprised when I met a cool, distinguished Ethiopian gentleman. His name was Kevin and he was a native Washingtonian. He had a charming accent and an infectious smile, and I could tell from the moment we met that we were going to be great friends.

Kevin and I quickly hit it off and would often sit for hours discussing all the ins and outs of living in DC. He was knowledgeable about the city's rich history and culture, and I loved hearing his stories about growing up in the area. He was also a student at the university, majoring in electrical engineering. I was fascinated by his academic pursuits and loved to listen to him talk about his future goals and aspirations.

Despite our busy schedules, Kevin and I always made time for each other. Whether it was grabbing a coffee or grabbing a bite to eat, we always had a great time together. I appreciated the fact that he was always there to lend an ear and offer a helping hand.

As the months went by, Kevin became like an older brother to me. He showed me the ropes of life in the city, introduced me to new people and experiences, and helped me navigate the challenges of college life. I am so grateful for our friendship, and I will always remember the impact that he had on my life.

One day, my parents came to visit me on campus, and a sophisticated gentleman noticed that they seemed lost while walking around. He offered to help them and introduced himself as Daniel. My mother told him that she was looking for her son, a tall and big gentleman, and Daniel immediately knew who they were talking about. He had a Jamaican New York accent, and I loved his vernacular as he was very well-spoken. That day, Daniel and I met, and we instantly hit it off. At the time, Daniel was working in the help desk in the IT department on campus and was also a student. Interestingly, both of us ended up applying for the same internship at IBM, which was looking for IT consultants.

Another day, as I was walking to class, I saw a beautiful young lady radiating positive energy. I had to stop and introduce myself, and she said her name was Lisa. I loved Lisa's style and how she dressed. She mentioned that her brother worked in the help desk, and I immediately put two and two together and asked if her brother was Daniel, to which she said yes. She also mentioned that their father was the Dean of Admissions, and I was amazed that it was a family affair. However, I did not ask for Lisa's number as I did not want to hit on my new friend's sister. I never told Daniel that I had a crush on his sister.

Daniel and I both had a passion for technology. It was a long process, but we both landed the job and it was a great experience. We learned so much from each other and had fun while doing it. We traveled to different parts of the DMV for projects and got to see so many new things.

One of my favorite memories with Daniel was when we were working on a project in Bethesda, MD, and he took me to this amazing Jamaican restaurant. The food was delicious, and I felt like I was transported to another world. I got to try all kinds of new dishes and drinks that I had never had before. We had a great time, and I felt like I was part of his Caribbean culture.

Calvin, Peter, Sampson, Josh, Greg, Kevin, Daniel, and I had some wild and crazy college stories. We all had different interests, backgrounds, and personalities, but one thing we all had in common was our love for good food and good times.

One day, we all decided to throw a massive college party. We spent hours cooking up a feast and planning games and activities. The day of the party finally arrived, and everything was going according to plan until... we ran out of plates.

In a panic, we started searching for plates and stumbled upon a stack of paper plates at the bottom of a pantry. In our excitement, we started using them to serve our food. But as the night went on and the partying continued, the paper plates started to get soggy and fall apart.

Soon, our once-delicious feast was reduced to a mess of food and paper plate fragments all over the floor. We couldn't stop laughing as we tried to clean up the mess, and we all agreed that it was the messiest and most unforgettable party we ever had.

From that day on, whenever we got together, we would tell the story of how we came so close to serving food without plates, and we would all roar with laughter, reminding us of the bonds that we had formed in college.

One day in our Critical Thinking class, we decided to pull a prank on our professor. The professor was known for her strict demeanor and never cracking a smile. She was tall, blonde, incredibly intelligent, but very stoic with a Russian accent.

Before class, we came up with a plan to make her laugh. During her presentation, I decided to raise my hand and ask her a question while impersonating her. To our surprise, the professor started chuckling hysterically. The students in the class were laughing so hard they were wiping tears from their eyes.

After the class ended, the professor approached me, still chuckling. She said, "I never thought I'd see the day when someone could make me laugh in class."

From that day on, our professor became a lot more relaxed and jovial, much to the delight of the rest of the class.

Everyone in the group became close friends after that day and had many more adventures and laughs throughout their college years. But the moment when I made the professor laugh will always be one of our favorite memories.

One of the greatest blessings that I attained in college was meeting some real down-to-earth people that come from so many parts of the globe and so many cultural experiences. I never had that growing up, and I love having diversity in my circle.

Even though I was this big, tall nerd in college, I still had no game whatsoever and didn't know how to talk to women. My social skills at this time were very inept, and I was deeply seeking any sort of remedial services I could get my hands on. Calvin gave me some really good advice. He said, "You should work part-time in a club. There are women all the time, and it's an easy place to just work that muscle and build it."

So I followed Calvin's advice and got a second job working in a club in downtown Washington, DC. He was right. It certainly did work that muscle. This was also my very first time experiencing what club life is all about. I've never seen so many people walking around happy, just randomly going around talking to random strangers they don't know, and I was so fascinated with just studying the human behavior of the whole experience. They assigned me to guard the stairs because I was working security, pretty much an easy job if you're a six-foot-four, two-hundred-and-fifty-pound guy.

As I stood there, watching the crowd below me, I couldn't help but be enamored by the energy in the room. The music was loud, the lights were flashing, and people were laughing, dancing, and having a good time. I was struck by how everyone seemed to be living in the moment, not caring about their worries or responsibilities.

I started to notice the different groups of people and how they interacted with each other. There were groups of friends, couples on dates. I was approached by a young woman who was trying to get up the stairs to the VIP section. I stopped her, explaining that she didn't have the proper wristband to enter. She begged and pleaded, claiming that she was with a VIP and needed to get up there. I was about to turn her away when she offered me a hundred dollars to let her pass. At first, I was hesitant, but then I thought about how much I could use the extra money. However, I couldn't accept it.

As I turned her away, I felt bad, but I started thinking of different scenarios in my head. What if she got caught? What if someone found out that I took a bribe? Eventually, the young woman returned, looking frazzled and upset. She explained that she had gotten into an altercation and needed to leave the club right away.

From that night on, I made a vow to never let money cloud my judgment. I was at the club to do a job, not to make extra cash on the side. I also learned the importance of being true to myself and my values, no matter the temptation.

As I arrived at work on Friday evening, I met this interesting and ravishing-looking young lady. She was gorgeous, tall, just how I like it, with a beautiful smile. I was instantly in love, but this time, I was going to introduce myself. I was not going to be Mr. Freeze. So, as she was standing next to me, I asked her if she was having a good time so far. She said yes and that the place was quite beautiful. I told her I absolutely agreed. I introduced myself and told her my name was Max.

She said, "I'm Jasmin."

In that moment, I started feeling like Aladdin, wanting to take her on a magic carpet ride. So we started talking, and she told me she was early for a birthday party that her cousin was hosting there. In the back of my mind, I thought, "If your cousin looks like you, you have a beautiful family."

We talked for a while, had some laughs, and I got so nervous to ask for her phone number. But when she said yes, I was over the moon. You don't even understand how I felt in that moment. I felt so accomplished. I had just landed my internship at IBM, and now I had met a beautiful woman the same week. I was jubilant. This was at happy hour, and I now see why they call it happy hour because I was happy the rest of the night.

As the night went on, the club started to fill up, and it became more hectic. People were getting more inebriated and rowdy, and I had to keep my guard up to make sure everything remained under control. But despite the chaos around me, I couldn't help but feel grateful for meeting Jasmin and having the chance to talk to her. I couldn't wait to call her and see where things would go between us.

The next day, I got home in the early hours of the morning and slept for about four hours. I woke up early and decided to call her. We talked for hours and really hit it off. She was smart, funny, and had a great sense of humor. She laughed at my jokes, and I loved our idiosyncrasies. She told me she was working on finishing up her Master's degree while working for a nonprofit downtown. I loved it. She was an educated, gorgeous, sapiosexual woman, just the kind of girl that my mother and family would be proud of me to be with. We both learned we had the same family values, and that was very huge for me. I loved that she was a very spiritual individual, just like my mother. We even talked about going to church together.

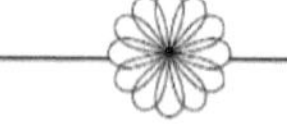

# Chapter 6

Entering the dating culture of the DMV was quite exciting for me. Firstly, I was going to be going out with someone who is from Maryland and who went to college at the University of Maryland. After the night that we met, we kept in contact, and then I decided to plan a date for us. At this time, I was a low-budget college kid, so I had to get creative, but I wanted to make it special. So, I planned a date for us to go to the Smithsonian Zoo. I had never been there, but I always liked being around animals. So, this was a great opportunity for me to really get to know her more. I was fascinated by her walk of life and intrigued to tell her about mine, since we instantly had a connection and bonded so well. Plus, I learned that we had something in common; she was fascinated with world travel just like I was. I could instantly open up and share with her like I never had before.

I've always been the type of person to date with purpose. When I'm getting to know someone, I ask myself, "Could I see a future with this person? What kind of mother would she be? Could she be strong like my mother during tough times?" Even though I was young, my friends and everyone told me I was an old soul.

They used to say, "You're well beyond your years."

They didn't understand the experiences I had growing up; I had to grow up fast.

It was a beautiful summer DMV evening, and the fish market was bustling with people. It was our second date, Jasmin, and I walked around, checking out the different seafood stalls and sampling some of the freshest seafood we had ever tasted. She was amazed by the variety of fish and shellfish, and I was just happy to be there with her.

We found a small restaurant by the water and decided to sit down and enjoy a meal together. The sun was setting and the view was breathtaking. We talked and laughed and enjoyed our meal, savoring every bite of the delicious seafood.

After dinner, we strolled along the waterfront, holding hands and taking in the sights and sounds of the city. It was a perfect evening, filled with happiness, and I knew that this was just the beginning of a long and very special.

From that moment on, Alexandria's fish market held a special place in our hearts, and we often returned there to reminisce about that wonderful evening and the love that brought us more closer together.

As we went on more dates, our bond became stronger. It was serendipitous that we had connected. We had built an amazing foundation of friendship before we became lovers, and I was enthralled with our situation. Her presence inspired me to be more than I ever thought I could be. Watching her pursue her Master's degree while I pursued my Bachelor's made me feel lucky to have such a beautiful and sapiosexual woman want to be with me.

I was thrilled to introduce Jasmin to my college friends, so I planned a night out for us. They all loved her immediately, just as I did. They often joined us on our adventures and outings, and together, we formed a tight-knit group of friends who always had each other's backs.

Calvin, Peter, Josh, Kevin, and Daniel became like brothers to Jasmin and I, and we loved spending time with them. They introduced us to new experiences and helped us grow as individuals. We started game night where we would play board games and have a great time.

As our relationship continued to grow and thrive, Jasmin and I knew that we had something special. With our close friends by our side, we were unstoppable and ready to conquer the world. Our love and friendship was truly a blessing and we cherished every moment we spent together.

At this time, I was just so blessed and fortunate things are going well in school, in my new relationship, and with work. Then on one afternoon my mother calls me she had informed me that my aunt had passed away and you should come home. I was so distraught my aunt and I were so close growing up.

As I sat there, I realized that this loss was a huge blow to me and I needed to take the time to process it properly. I was feeling a mix of sadness, anger, and emptiness all at once. I knew that it was going to take some time to come to terms with my aunt's passing and the fact that she was no longer going to be a part of my life.

I also knew that I had to be there for my mother, who was going through her own grief and loss. I packed my bags and set out on the long drive home, taking time to reflect on all the memories I had with my aunt and all the ways she had impacted my life.

When I arrived home, I was greeted by my family and friends who were all there to support me. They surrounded me with love and comfort, and together we began the process of grieving and honoring my aunt's life.

I realized that even though she was no longer with us physically, the love and memories we shared would always be a part of me. I felt grateful for all the blessings and good things that I still had in my life, and for the people who loved and supported me through it all.

She used to make such delicious brownies; I loved her sense of humor. She taught me the importance of money management. She would babysit me when my mom and father were working a lot. Her and my grandmother were too sick to attend my high school graduation. Now she won't be there for my college graduation. Another life lesson I learned never take those precious moments with your loved ones for granted cherish every minute to the last nanosecond.

While I was home, I spent time with my grandmother, who was not well. It took everything out of me not to get emotional, so I hugged my mom, dad, and all the family members who were there, including my cousins and church family. However, I couldn't stay in the house that night. There were too many memories of so many good moments, and I didn't want that moment to be the last one I remembered of my aunt. I learned in that moment with my family is when you lose someone that's close to you, you lose a piece of yourself that goes with them. I told my mom and father I can't stay here. I started thinking about memories of aunt, grandfather, and grandmother. It felt so different being back in the home I grew up in. It just didn't feel the same like during the time of growing up there. I immediately drove back to DC, I didn't have the emotional and psychological strength to attend my aunt funeral.

When I arrived back to DMV, Jasmin comforted me she was surprised to see me back so soon but I knew I could be completely vulnerable with her and be open and to tell her things that has never been easy for me to open up and talk about. As an only child I just internalized and deal with it on my own. She became Wonder Woman for me and comforted me.

A few months had passed, and Jasmin invited me to Baltimore, MD. She had a conference there for work and asked if I wanted to stay with her. Let me give you some backstory: this was going to be the first time we spent the night together. She's an old-school, classy type of girl that I love. I told her yes, and since I hadn't explored Baltimore before, I was excited to go. The moments leading up to meeting her, I was so nervous because I was thinking in the back of my mind that we were finally going to be intimate. As a Virgo perfectionist overthinker, I was nervous and wanted this moment to be perfect.

When I arrived at the Baltimore Inner Harbor, where we stayed, it was a beautiful day. After checking into the hotel, we went for a walk to get food. It was my first time visiting the ESPN Zone on the Inner Harbor. After we ate, we went to the bookstore next door, which was the biggest bookstore I had ever seen. As major bibliophiles, we found an interesting book to check out. Jasmin went to get coffee, and we sat down together at a table by the window with a picturesque view of the harbor and the city. In the back of my mind, I was looking at her, just admiring her beauty and thinking about all that I had learned about her. I couldn't even pay attention to my book, but that was the moment I knew I wanted to spend the rest of my life with this person.

Every moment of being around her was just so calm peaceful and serene. Her presence elevated my solitude and trust me every true man knows when he meets that one. The apple of his eye and she was definitely the one for me. She had a pure innocent spirit about her, all I wanted to do was just love and protect her. Then the Virgo perfection side of me starts to think just how am I going to get a ring and propose on this low budget lifestyle of mine. I didn't want no one else to have this woman I was going to figure out a way.

After we left the bookstore, we walked back to the hotel, and I was nervous all the way back she started to notice something was off about me. I had to put on this certain bravado of acting like everything was fine. Then she grabs me by the arm and holds my hand that just calmed me down and I relaxed. As we got back to the hotel room, she was like why don't you relax I'm just going to go take a shower I was like sure.

So I just got my suitcase and I started unpacking while she was in the shower to give me something to do to keep from getting nervous and then she walks out of the bathroom. She put on that sexy robe that they give you at the hotels and my mind went to places my mind shouldn't have went but it went there she was looking absolutely incredible like she always does. She looked at me and says why are you staring so hard like you've never seen a woman before? In my mind she don't know I've never seen a woman like her. I was so distracted watching her moisturize never actually seen her as she in this manner. This was more entertaining to me than floor seats at the Lakers watching Kobe and Shaq. She told me to take a shower and relax, and I obediently followed her orders like a new, trained dog getting acclimated to its owner. So after I finish my shower I realized that hotel robe was definitely not going to fit me so I just had to walk out with my towel on that barely went around my waist.

There she was, laying on the bed when I came out of the bathroom. It was a moment I will never forget. She was lying there like a Playboy centerfold, waiting for me. We both are big fans of Maxwell's music, so she had some playing in the background. She asked me if I was going to join her on the bed, and I was completely frozen where I was standing. She looked like a beautiful young, sexy Sade lying on the bed, and I was trying to act like a smooth operator, which was an epic fail. She whispered in my ear, "Was it worth the wait?"

We had been dating for six months at this point. I looked into her eyes and nodded, and for the rest of that night, we explored each other in ways we never had before. The chemistry between us was electric, and I felt like I was experiencing love for the first time. As the night passed, we talked, laughed, and simply enjoyed each other's company, and I knew that I had found something special with her. The next morning, as I woke up with her in my arms, I was filled with a sense of peace and contentment. I knew that I had found my soulmate, and that this was the start of a beautiful journey together. I could not keep my hands off her I was up the whole night holding her. I never imagined that I would fine my dream woman this soon in my life. Life taught me you have to expect the unexpected.

As I was lying in the bed, I started to have thoughts of wanting to propose to her. So many thoughts permeating in my mind of how I wanted to do it. Our connection was just on another metaphysical level, we reached a stage and there is no way I could ever wanted to lose this woman. At the time, I hadn't arrived where I wanted to be but I knew I would get there. Knowing that Jasmin was by my side I was going to go to a whole another level in life. I planned a date for us the next day to Fells Point. After we got breakfast that morning, we walked over there it was a beautiful sunny day a little windy but still beautiful nonetheless. We took a break and sat on the bench and just admire the view. We both love the simple pleasures of people watching and just the enjoyment of each other's company. That was the moment I got down on one knee and I asked her to marry me. I told her I don't have the ring just yet but I knew the one I want to get. I was afraid she was going to be upset that I am doing such a proposal without a ring, but she didn't care she still said yes. I was so happy in that moment that I have a fiancé.

    She was so excited and ecstatic in that moment she called, and her family and I called mine to share the news. It was just a glorious momentous occasion in both of our lives. We found the right chemistry, the right connection, the right bond plus we had so much in common it was like two soulmates that finally connected. We went back to the bookstore that day and she started buying wedding magazines.

# Chapter 7

Jasmin, a suburban girl from Southern Maryland and the youngest of five siblings. Her parents are smart, intellectual bourgeoisie, and met when her father was in the Air Force stationed in the United Kingdom. Her father was a hardworking man, very loving, and a great provider. Her mom mostly stayed at home and raised the kids, much like my mom. They had a passion for loving life and living it to the fullest. I was always mystified and intrigued at what made Jasmin who she was, and once I stepped into her world of getting to know her and her circle, it all made sense.

She grew up in a close-knit family that placed a strong emphasis on family values. Her parents instilled in her the importance of love, respect, and responsibility from a young age. Jasmin learned that family was not just about blood, but about the people who support you, care for you, and are always there for you no matter what. She saw the way her parents always put their family first and was determined to carry on that tradition in her own life.

As she grew older, Jasmin became known for her strong sense of family values. She was always there to support her loved ones and was never too busy to lend a helping hand. She took her responsibilities as a sister, daughter, and aunt seriously and always put her family first. She was so much like her mother; they're like best friends when you notice the chemistry between the two and when they're around each other. I would sit in her parents' house and just chuckle at the way they laughed and joked with each other.

When Jasmin started telling me about her upbringing, I realized we had so much in common. It felt like we were connected even when we were growing up. She was very smart in school, just like me, and had a fascination for books. She had a thirst for knowledge and adventure, and her family went on frequent trips when she was growing up.

I remember the first time I met her whole family. They were having a family reunion in Pennsylvania, where her father's family is from. I had the best time of my life at the family reunion. The food was amazing, and they were playing some good music. The vibe, energy, and chemistry amongst her family were just incredible. It reminded me a lot of my family. I'm an empath, so I can easily read people's energy from afar, and the energy was so stimulating and gravitating.

Jasmin played a lot of sports, and she was really good at field hockey. She was so good that after she graduated high school, she continued to play at the University of Maryland. She also did modeling, which intrigued me because I could definitely see it; she had the look.

The more I learned about her, the more intrigued I became. She was such a beautiful woman inside and out, with a beautiful soul. She wasn't arrogant or pretentious; she always remained humble, and I loved that about her.

Jasmin is a person who is known for being down to earth. This means that she is genuine, authentic, and has a realistic view of the world. She is not easily impressed by material possessions or status, and instead values meaningful relationships and experiences. Some of the specific characteristics that make Jasmin a down to earth person and why I loved her so much.

Empathy, Jasmin has a natural ability to understand and relate to other people's feelings and perspectives. She is a good listener and is always there to offer support and advice to those in need.

Humility, Jasmin is humble and does not boast about her accomplishments or put herself on a pedestal. She is grateful for what she has and always strives to help others.

Practicality, Jasmin is a practical person who is grounded. She can see situations and problems clearly and find practical solutions to them.

Open-mindedness, Jasmin is open-minded and is always willing to listen to other people's opinions and perspectives. She does not judge others and is accepting of people from all walks of life.

Simplicity, Jasmin values simplicity and does not seek extravagance or material possessions. She is content with the simple things in life and finds joy in the everyday moments.

Those traits make Jasmin a beloved and respected person who is always there for others. People feel comfortable around her because she is approachable, kind, and genuine.

She was always the type that could easily make friends and you could truly see that. If you are a friend with her and she considered, you a friend you were going to be a friend for life. Those kinds of people are just rare they're like rubies. It made me so extremely honored that she wanted me to be a part of her life in any form or capacity. Knowing she selected me to be her fiancé as someone she could see spending the rest of her life with it's the highest honor.

My mom and father had told me that when a man finds a good wife, he finds a good thing and they were right.

The moment I met her friends I absolutely thought they were adorable Ashley and Danielle were just incredible and I see why they had a long history of being close friends. It was like you saw certain parts of Jasmin in them and now I see what bonded them so well.

She shared with me a funny story of her family taking a road trip. They all decided to play their favorite song, The Power by Snap. Everyone got into the groove and began singing along, their voices ringing out over the countryside.

When they reached the Pennsylvania state line, their singing got even louder. Jasmin's brother started jumping up and down in the van and her mom started waving her hands in the air. Even her father got into the fun, nodding his head and tapping his hands on the steering wheel. Jasmin felt like she was in some kind of music video, and it was a moment she'd never forget. The family continued singing The Power all the way to their destination, and the fun didn't end when they arrived. For Jasmin, that road trip and the song that made it so special, were a reminder that the power of music is something to cherish.

We both started laughing so hard, I can so relate to that because I told her my father loved listening to "Too Close" by Next all the way to Chicago on our road trip.

During this phase of getting to know her it made me realize that the person that's meant for you sometimes you guys are going to start building memories that you can easily relate to when your paths cross. I don't know if that's true or not, but it's certainly felt that way.

Jasmin always loved spending time in the kitchen with her mother, watching her cook delicious meals for the family. She would often ask her mother about the ingredients and techniques she used, but her mother would simply say, "You'll learn when you're older."

As Jasmin grew up and moved out on her own. One day, she decided she wanted to learn how to cook just like her mother. She called her mother and asked for a cooking lesson.

Her mother was overjoyed and agreed to come over and teach her everything she knew. For the next few weeks, Jasmin and her mother spent hours in the kitchen, cooking and experimenting with different recipes.

Jasmin's mother taught her about the importance of using fresh ingredients and the right spices to enhance the flavor of the dish. She also taught her the secret to her famous sauces and how to make the perfect pie crust.

With each lesson, Jasmin grew more confident in the kitchen, and soon she was able to cook meals that were just as delicious as her mother's. She felt proud of her new skills and couldn't wait to share her creations with her family.

Jasmin was always envious of her older brother's athletic abilities. He was a star on his school's basketball and football teams, and Jasmin wished she could be just as good.

One day, her brother offered to teach her how to play basketball. Jasmin was hesitant at first, but she knew this was her chance to improve her skills and impress her brother.

They spent countless hours in the driveway, with her brother teaching her how to dribble, shoot, and pass. At first, Jasmin struggled and often missed the ball, but her brother never gave up on her. He encouraged her to keep practicing and never made her feel embarrassed by her mistakes.

With each passing day, Jasmin began to feel more confident on the court. She started making shots and even began to play a little rough and tumble, just like her brother.

Soon, Jasmin found that she loved playing basketball and was even better than she ever imagined. She started playing on the school team and found a new passion for sports.

Jasmin never forgot the lessons she learned from her brother. He taught her that with hard work and perseverance, anyone could become good at sports. And she was grateful for the opportunity to learn from the best.

Jasmin always looked up to her older sister. She was intelligent, confident, and had a passion for helping others. Jasmin admired her sister's ability to handle any situation with grace and ease and wished she could be more like her.

One day, her sister noticed Jasmin's admiration and offered to mentor her. She wanted to help Jasmin find her own path in life and become the best version of herself.

They spent hours talking about their goals, dreams, and aspirations. Jasmin's sister taught her about the importance of hard work, self-confidence, and being kind to others. She also showed her how to handle difficult situations and make the right decisions.

Jasmin was grateful for her sister's guidance and took her advice to heart. She started making positive changes in her life and found that she was becoming more confident and self-assured.

With each passing day, Jasmin grew more and more like her sister. She found her own passion for helping others and became known for her kindness and compassion.

Jasmin always looked up to her father. He was hardworking, dedicated, and had a strong work ethic. He worked long hours to support the family and always put his family first, no matter what.

Growing up, Jasmin often watched her father at work and was inspired by his dedication and commitment. She admired his ability to handle challenges with ease and was determined to follow in his footsteps.

One day, Jasmin approached her father and asked for his advice on how to become more productive and efficient. Her father was overjoyed that she was interested in his work and offered to teach her everything he knew.

They spent hours talking about the importance of setting goals, prioritizing tasks, and staying focused. Her father taught her that success was not just about working hard, but also about working smart. He showed her how to balance her time and energy to achieve maximum results.

She was grateful for her father's guidance and took his advice to heart. She started applying his lessons to her own life and soon found that she was becoming more productive and successful.

She was a true Sagittarius, a vibrant free spirit with an insatiable thirst for adventure. She was always eager to explore new places, meet new people, and try new things. She lived life to the fullest and refused to be held back by anything or anyone.

Growing up, Jasmin's family and friends were always amazed by her energy and enthusiasm. She had a magnetic personality that drew people to her and a contagious smile that could light up a room.

Despite her carefree spirit, Jasmin was also fiercely independent and determined. She was never afraid to take risks and chase her dreams, no matter how big or bold they may be.

Jasmin's travels took her to some of the most exotic and exciting places in the world. She climbed mountains, swam with dolphins, and danced under the stars. Through each adventure, she gained a deeper appreciation for life and a better understanding of herself.

I was so proud of her for all the decisions that she made early in her life to get her to where she is to the point where I paths have crossed. Now as I was getting to know her, she was teaching me things and I was teaching her things. We began empowering each other she became more of her divine feminine she fed my divine masculine.

# Chapter 8

Her and I started planning the transition of living together so at this time she was living in Maryland and I was living in Virginia so she's decides to move to Virginia with me. We had a cute little seven hundred square foot apartment, it was not much but this was going to be my very first time living with someone and sharing closet space and so much other space that I didn't even think about.

Learning what it's like living with a woman and the woman I love at that. On move in day, we encountered several unexpected issues. We were trying to navigate how we were going to accommodate all of her clothes in the limited closet space. We had the funniest experience of trying to move our new furniture, we bought a new L-shaped couch I don't know what we were thinking, and we had a cute garden style apartment there was no way we could get this up the third floor. My college friends was trying to help us. This is how I knew my friends were real is when you call and ask them can you help us move.

We had a bit of a struggle when it came to sharing the same bathroom. We soon realized that our different morning routines and bathroom habits were causing some conflict.

For starters, Jasmin was an early riser and was always up before me, she spent a great deal of time in the bathroom every morning. This meant that I had to rush to get ready for work and often found myself feeling rushed and stressed.

On the other hand, I was a bit of a neat freak and couldn't stand the mess that Jasmin left behind in the bathroom after she was finished. Makeup all over the counter, hair all over the floor, and towels thrown on the floor were just some of the things that drove me crazy. I had some wild habits too that drove her crazy, working two jobs and school full-time. My snoring was ruthless I'm sure she felt like she was sleep next to King Kong. I'll admit when I got home sometimes, I was just ravenous and exhausted.

We soon realized that something had to be done, so we sat down and had a talk about our bathroom habits. We agreed to establish a set routine for the bathroom and set some rules for keeping it clean and organized.

To our surprise, these small changes made a big difference. Our mornings were now much more relaxed and stress-free, and the bathroom was always clean and tidy.

We learned that communication and compromise are key when it comes to living together, and the challenges that we faced in the bathroom helped us to grow as a couple. We now look back on those times with a smile and appreciate the lessons that we learned from our shared bathroom experience.

Solving Closet Space

I had to come up with a solution to solve our closet situation. I never knew the extent of her clothing collection, including shoes, accessories, and purses.

For our first week, we still had items in boxes until we were able to take a trip to the furniture store to find some solutions. We bought a chest that I had to assemble, and once we got it home, it took me over three hours to put it together. I helped her fold some clothes and load them into the chest, which helped create more closet space for us to share.

Two nights later, after Jasmin and I had gotten ready for bed, we had turned out the lights, said goodnight to each other, and were just cuddling in bed. Suddenly, the chest collapsed, making the loudest sound that I thought it had woken up everyone in the apartment building. We looked at each other and just started laughing. I guess we overstocked it with too many clothes. How in the world could this have happened to us all within the first week of living together?

Jasmin looks at me and ask Are you sure you put this together as it was instructed? I followed the instructions, in the back of my mind at least I thought I did.

I felt embarrassed. I didn't want Jasmin to think, "Oh my God, I can't fix anything."

The more I tried to solve some of our issues, the more problems I seemed to create. The next morning, I got on the phone and told my father what had happened. He started chuckling and then said, "Don't be so hard on yourself. When I was your age, I was making all kinds of mistakes when I first started living on my own."

He gave me one of the best pieces of advice that I will never forget. He said, "In life, it's not about what you go through, it's about how you get through it."

# Yoga

Jasmin and I were known as the "fit couple" among our friends. We were always encouraging each other to stay healthy and active, but sometimes our competitive nature got the best of us.

Jasmin tells me you need to start working on your flexibility, I was somewhat offended but in the back of my mind she was right. She invited me to come to yoga with her, this was my very first time ever doing yoga. She brings me to take Bikram yoga, and I asked her what was like why is it so hot in here? she tells me it's part of the experience keep an open mind, in the back of my mind I'm trying to make sure I don't pass out and collapse in here. So as the instructor walks in she locks the door, I was not aware that once the session has started you can't leave. I could not believe that I had to stay in here for an hour with no water. I felt like Jasmin was punishing me, I begin to sit on my mat just try to relax my mind. I was sweating profusely I had never sweat this much in my life. I was the only male in the room so I was trying to not act weak, but I looked at these women like they were Navy Seals and you can tell they were not novices at all. How could they do this on a regular basis but then I started to notice as I'm trying to do a Down Dog they had immense flexibility. I felt like I was watching Cirque du Soleil in a classroom setting. After the session was over I had a new profound respect not only for Jasmin but for the individuals that could do that on a regular basis. The experience reminded me about learning to keep an open mind and stepping outside of your comfort zone.

Jasmin and I remained to be fitness buddies we would go to the gym every day but I realize she was determined to look good for our wedding. I was strength training she was doing her calisthenics, weight training, and cardio. I would look at her at the gym at times, I didn't know if she was training for our wedding or was she training for the Olympics. She would be running on that treadmill like she was Gail Devers or Jackie Joyner-Kersey. She would always cook so many healthy dishes, I never ate so many vegetables in my life. I loved every minute of it I was getting healthier I was feeling good about myself. She also introduced me to one of her mother's English traditions I had never drank so many different types of tea, she had tea all the time.

One of the things that I loved about living with Jasmin she always captivated my attention. I was just sitting on the couch, and I had invited Daniel over and we were just watching LeBron play completely mystified by his style of play. Jasmin cooked dinner for us, and she brings our plates to us in the living room. She goes and sets back down at her desk to do some work, in that moment I just could not stop looking at her. I just loved how much she made our home a happy home.


## Mouse Story


We were unpacking boxes and getting everything in order when suddenly, Jasmin shrieked. "What's wrong?" I asked, running over to her.

"I just saw a mouse!" Jasmin exclaimed.

I was skeptical. "Are you sure? Maybe it was just a shadow."

But Jasmin was certain. "I know what I saw. It was definitely a mouse."

I grabbed a flashlight, and we set out on a mission to catch the mouse. I searched high and low but couldn't find it. Just when I was about to give up, I heard a tiny rustling sound coming from the pantry.

Jasmin bravely volunteered to open the pantry door, and I stood ready with the flashlight. When Jasmin opened the door, the mouse scurried out, and I shined the flashlight on it, trying to get a better look.

In the process, we both stumbled and ended up in a pile on the floor. We were laughing so hard we could barely stand up.

Jasmin didn't know I was scared to capture that mouse, so I called my friend Greg, who lived close by. I knew the Marine had a solution for how to capture it. He rushed over and brought a shoebox. Next thing you know, within about the first 10 minutes of him arriving, the mouse was on a sticky pad in a shoebox. It's always good to have a Marine in your inner circle.

That week, I receive a phone call from my mom that my grandmother had passed away. My grandmother was one of the strong matriarchs of the family she would recycle soda cans and sell them put that money towards my college fund. I had to reach deep down and try to be strong I knew it wasn't going to be easy for me. When I went home this time to see my family as Jasmin and I was driving down I was thinking about all the good memories as a kid growing up. Riding in the back seat with my grandparents on the way to the grocery store and to so many different places. We used to love having donuts fresh glaze especially when the hot red sign was on. My grandmother is the one who introduced me to Spam. She was such an amazing cook she used to make something called a Brown Sugar pie it was a family secret recipe and those pies were so amazing. She could do all of this cooking walking around the house, and she couldn't see. My grandparents and my parents' marriage inspired me to want to have a long happy marriage.

I'm so intrigued at where life is going to take me now that I have a partner, best friend, and lover. Even though I lost so much in the same year I gained so much as well. After we laid my grandmother to rest I came back to Northern Virginia not sad because what I lost is now living within me and their spirit lives there forever. I see my various parts of my grandmother and aunt in Jasmin.

A few days after we returned, Jasmin tells me we are going to see visit her parents. She tells me you're going to sat outside and talk with my father, I want him to get to know you and understand why I love you. I got nervous because I knew I didn't ask for his daughter's hand and I was like Oh my he might be upset with me I was very nervous. We drove down to her parents place, I loved her family her mom's lovely English accent and her father's Pennsylvania accent. I had a strong affinity to him also retired military very successful computer nerd just like myself, so we instantly had a connection. We will talk about mainframes that were popular in his day and I would tell him about servers and things that I would do.

So when we met that day I sat down with him on the front porch not instantly apologized for not asking his hand I was hoping he would just spare me any lapses in decorum. He was a laid-back reasonable guy he just wanted to know if I was going to take care of his daughter. I looked at him dead in his eyes it was probably the one of the most serious moments I've ever had, and I made that commitment to him that she was going to be fine I was going to do everything in my power to keep her happy because she's done such a good job of taking care of me. I learned in that moment that he was passing the baton to me all of his life that was his duty was to protect and provide and now that responsibility falls on me. I was honored and we stood up and went inside and her mom was serving us some Creme Brulee.

As Jasmin and I adjusted to living together I learned in this moment the importance of learning things about yourself you never knew until someone else points it out. The importance of making sure the toilet seat stays down. She would call me out on my selfishness, and the importance of sharing I never had to share growing up this is my first time. We were both sharing a bathroom a kitchen you don't have much space to yourself. This is when I learn "I" now becomes "we" it certainly was a hard adjustment for me. We had to overcome several obstacles but she could easily empathize and understand why I was the way I was because breaking from some bad habits but she loved me through it.

As the holidays were approaching this was our first time as an engaged couple going to have Thanksgiving at our parents' house and both of our moms cooked an amazing spread. I absolutely loved it but Jasmin was watching what she was eating because she was training like she was getting ready to join the Team USA Women's soccer team even though it was just a wedding. I understood because the perfectionist nature of myself really could relate so I mostly did a lot of the eating for us.

So for the next several months I'm focused on school and work she's focused on wedding planning training hard in the gym like I've never seen before.

We decided we were going to take a break and we were going to go to Miami. This was our first trip together; this was also my very first time taking a plane ride so I was very excited. Before we left for Miami, I finally saved enough money and got her the ring I had my eye on. She was thrilled at how beautiful it was. It was a Platinum Princess cut diamond ring she was excited to be showing it off while in her bikini in Miami.


Miami


The moment we landed in Miami we decided that we were going to stay in South Beach on Ocean Drive. I absolutely love the culture with the Art Deco design buildings we had a lovely hotel room facing right on the beach. I'll never forget our first day after we get something to eat, she was excited to put her bikini on and let's get to the beach. She look so good on that trip so many men were turning their necks and looking at her. All that hard work she's putting in the gym was taking her body to a whole another level. I'm walking alongside of her seeing all these men look at her and I was like yeah that's mine thank you very much.

So as we were heading to the beach, she mentioned that she wants to get some coffee so I found a Cuban place that served Cuban coffee. Now I am not a coffee drinker, but I was going to keep an open mind try something new. I did not realize that Cuban coffee is served in these small cups so after we both sampled it I will say it may have been only no more than about 15 to 20 minutes after it went in my system. That coffee was so strong I did not sleep for the entire weekend I didn't realize that I had such a caffeine sensitivity. Anywhere she wanted to go I had so much energy and was ready.

That trip had so many amazing memories of trying different food and experiencing the Miami culture. I had never experienced that kind of humidity my entire life my skin was so moisturized the entire trip. At the end of our trip I told her I am so looking forward to our wedding day and having more memories like this with you.

During this time of our lives my parents had told me they're going to be moving closer to Washington DC, so they resided in Fredericksburg VA. So, I was very ecstatic about having them closer spending more time with them but shortly after they arrived and moved in my father drives up to come visit us. As soon as my father arrives, he became very ill and very sick I didn't know what was going on I was very scared but luckily the hospital was just up the street from where we lived so I took him to the ER. I was so afraid and that moment that I was going to lose him his hypertension was severely elevated and the doctor said he had another stroke.

So in the midst of me finishing up school, being engaged, wedding planning, my father gets sick. I'm very fortunate and blessed and thankful that my mother was close my uncle was there and Jasmin family were there to support us. During these tough times I've experienced through life is just having the right loving and supportive people around you makes the most difficult times easier to shoulder.

So while my father was in the hospital recovering and progressing we still had a wedding to plan we had to get a venue locked down, meet with the caterers, put down all the deposits and then I still had to book our honeymoon. Another thing, I love about Jasmin and I we were a great team we were able to get it all done at times it was stressful, but we didn't let it get the best of us because we were just too happy and excited about starting married life together.

Interviewing the Wedding Planner

Jasmin and I were planning their dream wedding and were on the hunt for the perfect wedding planner. We had a list of candidates and were excited to start the interview process.

The first interview was with a wedding planner named Lily. Lily was energetic and confident, and she seemed to have a plan for everything. Jasmin and I were impressed, but we wanted to keep our options open and decided to keep interviewing other planners.

Next up was a wedding planner named Ashley. Ashley was more laid back, and her approach to planning was more relaxed. She emphasized the importance of enjoying the process and not getting too bogged down with details. We appreciated her perspective, but we wanted someone who was a bit more organized.

Finally, we met with a wedding planner named Grace. Grace was a seasoned professional, with years of experience and a wealth of knowledge. She listened intently to Jasmin's vision and offered creative solutions that we had never even considered.

By the end of the interview, Jasmin and I knew that Grace was the right wedding planner for them. We hired her on the spot, and she quickly got to work, putting together the wedding.

## Interview the Caterers

Jasmin and I were in the final stages of wedding planning, and one of their top priorities was finding the perfect caterer. We had a list of caterers to interview and were eager to sample some of their cuisine.

Our first stop was at a catering company run by a chef named Pierre. Chef Pierre was passionate about his food and eager to share his creations with Jasmin and I. We were blown away by the flavors and presentation of the dishes he presented to them, but they wanted to keep their options open and try more caterers.

Next, we visited a catering company run by a chef named Maria. Chef Maria's specialty was farm-to-table cuisine, and she used only the freshest ingredients in her dishes. Jasmin and I were impressed by the unique flavors and healthy options, but they wanted something a little more classic for their wedding.

Finally, they visited a catering company run by a chef named Jack. Jack was a seasoned professional, and he had been catering weddings for years. He presented to us with a range of classic dishes that he had perfected over time. We were so impressed by the taste and presentation of the food, and we looked at each and knew we had found the right caterer.

## Interviewing the DJ

We decided to interview a two potential DJs to get a better idea of who we should hire.
Jasmin and I were brimming with anticipation as we entered small club downtown. We were here to interview the DJ for our wedding.

The DJ was a small, wiry man with an easy smile and a ready laugh. We began asking our questions, starting with what kind of music he usually played. He told us that he usually played a wide variety of music genres, but he liked to specialize in electronic dance music. He also told us that he could create unique remixes to make the perfect wedding soundtrack.

We asked him what he thought made a successful wedding experience, and he told us that it was all about the energy and atmosphere. He said that it was important to have a good mix of music that appealed to all ages and that kept the energy level high throughout the evening.

Finally, we asked him what challenges he often faced when working at a wedding. He told us that he usually had to work with limited space, limited time, and limited resources. He also said that he often had to work with customers who had very specific music requests that may be difficult to fulfill.

At the end of the interview, we thanked the DJ for his time and asked him to keep us updated on the progress of our wedding soundtrack. He smiled, shook our hands, and said he would be in touch soon.

It was a sunny day when Jasmin and I arrived at the venue for our interview with a renowned DJ. We were both a little nervous and excited to hear from them about the music they'd be playing at the wedding. We greeted them and they welcomed us with a smile.

He shared how they got their start in the music industry, and their love for creating the perfect atmosphere and energy for a special occasion. He said he's been playing and mixing music for decades and always love the challenge of creating something that will make a wedding memorable.

As we continued talking, they showed us some of their signature mixes, and described how he create the perfect balance of music to keep the crowd entertained and engaged. He also shared some of their favorite moments from past weddings, where they felt they really made a difference in the atmosphere and the experience for everyone involved.

We thanked the DJ for their time and left feeling inspired and excited for the wedding. We knew the music would be a major highlight, and we couldn't wait to hear the special mix the DJ had prepared for us.

## Interview the Photographer and Videographer

We were very nervous about hiring the right photographer and videographer. We wanted to make sure we were getting the best professional possible. We decided to interview a few potential photographers and videographers that were recommended by Jasmin coworkers to get a better idea of who we should hire.

The first person we interviewed was an experienced photographer and videographer who had worked on over 100 weddings. We asked her to explain his process, his fees, and what type of coverage he provides. She was incredibly knowledgeable, and we felt like he could really capture the essence of our special day. she explained that he charges a flat fee and that he provides full coverage of the ceremony, reception, and any other related events. She also described his editing process and showed us some samples of his work. Plus, I loved her dog it was beautiful friendly Alaskan Malamute who really like me.

The second person we interviewed was a newer photographer and videographer. He had only worked on a few weddings, but we liked his style and thought he could provide a unique perspective. He started off by talking about his approach and his understanding of the importance of capturing candid moments. He also explained his editing process and showed us some of his work. We thought he was a great option, but ultimately decided to go with the more experienced photographer and videographer because of the breadth of her experience.

In the end, we were able to find the perfect photographer and videographer for our wedding. We felt confident in our decision and look forward to seeing the end results. With their help, we're sure our special day will be captured in all its beauty.

Game Night

During this time I loved how much our parents we're becoming like best friends especially since they were there supporting my mom as my father was recovering. So Jasmin and I were hosting a game night with our parents and decided to play a variety of games. My mom needed this we all wanted to have a good night of some laughter.

The evening started with a heated round of Pictionary, which had everyone in stitches.

Next up was Monopoly, and things took a turn for the dramatic. Jasmin's father was relentless in his pursuit of property, while my mom was making some questionable business deals. The room was filled with laughter and jeers as the game went on.

The real highlight of the night was when they played Scrabble. Our parents, who were initially hesitant to play, ended up having a blast and weren't afraid to get a little risqué. Then my father announced he was going to introduce us to the book of knowledge. I was quite intrigued I know my father is very smart.

As the night came to a close, everyone was in high spirits and feeling like kids again. We all agreed that we needed to have more game nights and that the next one would have to be even wilder.

# Planning the Honeymoon

Jasmin had put me in charge of planning the entire honeymoon. She did not want any parts of it, she did not want to provide any input I had complete autonomy. So the pressure was on but I had saved up a lot for this occasion.

Jasmin and I had been dreaming of our honeymoon for months. I had decided on the gorgeous Mayan Riviera of Mexico for the perfect romantic getaway.

It included the breathtaking view from our balcony in a luxurious resort swimming in the crystal clear waters of the Caribbean, exploring ancient Mayan ruins tucked away in the jungle, and sunsets spent nursing margaritas from the beach.

I had saved up for months working two jobs was paying off nicely and had set aside enough money to ensure that we could indulge in all the lavish experiences that the Riviera had to offer. I wanted to make this trip truly special. I also booked a private boat tour to take us along the coast and had made reservations at a Michelin-starred restaurant for a romantic dinner.

Finally, I reserved several days were filled with adventure and romance. Lastly, I wanted us to lounge on the beach, she could snorkeled in the warm waters since I can't swim, and explored the mysterious ruins.

# Bachelorette Party

Ashley, Danielle, and Jasmin were planning the bachelorette party. Jasmin was excited to celebrate with her two best friends, but they were having a tough time deciding what to do.

Ashley suggested they go to a wine tasting, but Danielle was afraid they would get too drunk and embarrass themselves. Jasmin then proposed they go to a spa for a relaxing day, but Ashley and Danielle both let out a collective snore.

In the end, they decided to go to a cooking class. Jasmin was excited to learn how to cook something new and Ashley and Danielle were excited for the free food. However, things quickly went wrong when they were asked to prepare a dish as a team. Ashley burned the garlic, Danielle couldn't chop the onions without crying, and Jasmin kept adding the wrong ingredients.

Despite their cooking disaster, the three friends ended up having a blast and laughed about their culinary mishap for years to come. The bachelorette party was a success, and Jasmin learned that the most important thing was spending time with her friends, no matter what they did.

Later that night, they decided to bar hop. They had never tried Petron Tequila before and were feeling adventurous, so they ordered a few rounds of shots.

They each took a shot and immediately regretted it. The tequila was strong, and they all started to feel the effects almost immediately after three rounds. Ashley started slurring her words and Danielle couldn't stop giggling. Jasmin, on the other hand, was feeling confident and challenged some new friends they met to a tequila chugging contest.

Their new friends who was used to drinking Petron Tequila all the time, accepted the challenge and they both started chugging. Jasmin was keeping up with the them shot for shot, until she suddenly stopped and exclaimed, "Wait a minute, is this even alcohol or just liquid fire?"

They couldn't stop laughing and told her it was indeed tequila. Jasmin, Ashley, and Danielle all started laughing and couldn't stop for what felt like hours. They left the bar, stumbling and giggling, with a newfound appreciation for Petron Tequila.

She called me to come pick them up, I was glad to hear from her it was so late that night. When I saw her stumbling and laughing outside the bar as I pulled the car over to help them get inside. I dropped her friends off and everyone was laughing and talking about how much fun they had. Jasmin was in the front seat telling me how much she loves me and can't wait to get married. This was my first meeting inebriated Jasmin but I loved what I was hearing. When we arrived home I knew I was going to always joke with her about this night and this would be our little inside joke.

At the rehearsal dinner this was the first time our families and friends were finally going to have a big get together. As we all were beginning to sat down and I was at the head of the table her parents and my parents I'm looking at each other smiling excited. I saw my father get emotional while talking to her father and my father tells him "thank you." and it was in that moment I knew our families were going to be united for a long time. I had wished my grandparents and my aunt was there but even though they weren't I felt like they were angels blessing me with a new family.

Night before the Wedding

It was the night before the wedding my friends and I decided to get together and they were going to host the party for me. I really wasn't interested in having some big bachelor party but I was like ok whatever you guys wanted to do I'm down. My friends know I don't drink and not a real big party guy and I'm the friend you call when you need a designated driver. Another thing that Jasmin loved about me I was told that we were like and old soul even though we were so young.

We went out for dinner and then we decided to bar hop along U street corridor. This was a fascinating place because that was one spot that had live jazz another spot they had reggae music and I loved just being part of something I never thought I would ever experience. There were people dancing in the street you could hear the music as you were walking. That was the night my friends and I we solidified our bond and I thank them for celebrating in this moment with me. Calvin pulls me aside and he asked me a direct question, "Are you sure you're ready to do this? We all love Jasmin she is a uniquely beautiful and one-of-a-kind. You're so young to be getting married." In the back of my mind, I was so surprised that he would ask me this the night before my wedding but I appreciate him being transparent about what he was thinking and feeling. He made me wonder am I doing this too soon there were so many questions in my mind. I started to go back and think about the reasons why I'm convinced I wanted to do it, he didn't know how Jasmin made me feel. I had never looked at another woman the way I look at her. I couldn't imagine my life without her. I responded to him by saying if you only knew how blessed and wonderful my life is since she came into it you would be doing the same thing. He just looked at me and smiled and said I'm happy for you.

## Wedding Day

It was September 11th, 2004, it's a day that will live in infamy for our nation, but it was also a special day for her and I. I could hardly hold my excitement. It had been 24 hours since I had last seen my bride,

My friends were my Groomsmen, and my best man is my long-time best friend Branden from Kindergarten. As we were getting ready in the hotel, I just took a moment and looked at all of them and I thank them for being with me on this special day. Shortly after I had said my speech, I get a phone call from her mother I was very nervous, her mother tells me we have a big problem the first thing that came to my mind Jasmin had cold feet. It turns out she left the wedding shoes at our place, and this was two hours before the wedding. I immediately rushed to my car and hoping and praying there was no traffic on a Saturday afternoon on the Beltway in Washington DC. Luckily, it only took me just little over forty-five minutes to do a round trip to get the shoes. Out of everything that we planned, and we went over the checklist several times we forgot the shoes.

I couldn't wait to finally see her walking down the aisle towards me, radiant in her wedding dress.

This is how imagined our wedding day, I had already played out the moment hundreds of times. I pictured the look of joy on her face as she joined me at the altar, the way her eyes would light up as I asked her to be my wife. I imagined the way the sun would shine through the windows and the sound of our family and friends cheering as we said our vows.

The sun shone brightly as Jasmin, and I said our vows of love and dedication to each other. We had promised to spend the rest of our lives together, and now we were fulfilling that promise.

I could hardly wait to take her in my arms and start our life together as husband and wife. I felt nothing but joy as I said my vows, making a promise to love her forever. Nothing else mattered except the fact that we were together at last.

The ceremony was perfect, and the guests were elated for us. I could see the love and joy on Jasmin's face, and it made my heart swell with joy. We both knew that this was the start of a beautiful journey together.

As the guests high-fived us and showered us with congratulations, we made our way to the reception. We spent the evening dancing, laughing, and celebrating with our closest friends and family.

How I imagined it wasn't even as good as reality. The day turned out perfectly even better than I had imagined in my mind. It was such a beautiful venue a beautiful day the sun the weather was perfect no humidity because I was worried that we were going to be sweating profusely but it was only 70 degrees for an outdoor wedding. The groomsmen and I arrived it was a place call Newton White Mansion a retired Admirals home had been donated to wedding venues. I love this place it was on a golf course the backdrop was beautiful, our wedding planner did a phenomenal job making sure everything was in order.

Then the ceremony begins, as I'm walking down the aisle I'm smiling at both families I saw my parents and her mother. I looked up at the cello being played I loved listening to classical music it always helped me relax. As I stood by the pastor seeing everybody begin to stand up and there she was slowly walking down the aisle with her father I had begun to shed a tear of joy and happiness.

I was just thanking God that I feel like the luckiest man in Washington DC. Her and I looked at each other just as jubilant as ever, I'm trying to take in every minute of this moment. As I take her by the hand I took a long deep breath and I said to her silently, "Are you ok?"

She just nodded her head, so after we recited our vows and the moment when the preacher said you may kiss the bride. I was so happy I married my dream girl how many guys can really say that.

I'm walking with my wife back inside the mansion we found a room where we could get some private time together and just take it all in and then the photographer and videographer walks in we only had maybe a minute and thirty seconds of private time. Then they wanted our parents to come in and they wanted to take pictures with them. I was so happy to see our parents they look like best friends for a long time every time I see them, they're always laughing and joking.

Then it was time for dinner and as they introduced us and Mr. and Mrs. Everyone was giving us a standing ovation clapping or shouting happy for us. Her and I were so happy we could finally sit down at our table and get ready to eat I don't think we had eaten for hours. It seemed like every five or 10 minutes someone was ringing the bell trying to get us to kiss. Then my father stands up as the DJ begins to play some music, so he broke the ice getting on the dance floor with my aunt. I was so happy that he got a chance to recover from his second stroke and be in this moment to celebrate this joyous occasion.

The reception was in full swing when the DJ finally announced the bride and groom's first dance. The lights dimmed and the guests waited in anticipation as the instrumental version of Stevie Wonder's classic "Ribbon In The Sky" started playing.

As Bride and Groom we stepped onto the dance floor and took each other's hand. They held each other tight as they moved gracefully to the music. They knew they had to make this moment last, and they were determined to make this wedding dance one to remember.

We swayed to the music, taking in the beauty of the moment. For us, it felt like a dream come true. Jasmin had always wanted to dream of having the first dance with the man she loved and now she was. I was moved that I was married to my dream girl.

When the song ended, the guests cheered in applause. We were beaming with joy, and the beauty of the moment was obvious. They had just shared their first dance as husband and wife and it was something they would remember forever.

Everyone was having a wonderful time. Little did they know that the wedding would get even better when the DJ announced that the soul train line was about to start. Immediately, all the guests started to get excited.

We were the first couple to get on the dance floor and our parents followed behind us. Everyone was having a great time, singing and dancing to the music.

The best part was when our fathers took the mic and encouraged everyone to clap as the soul train line got bigger and bigger. Everyone was laughing and having an enjoyable time as the soul train line circled the dance floor, with some people even getting up on chairs and tables.

After the music stopped, everyone was exhausted but still in great spirits. We thanked everyone for joining in the fun and wished everyone a great evening. As the guests left, we couldn't help but smile and think of the memorable time they had dancing in the soul train line.

As happy as they were for us I was so happy for them that we created a happy moment for them to bring all the people we love and cared about together. I wanted to make sure the photographer and videographer got all of this on video. I knew I was going to the replay that video for years to come of this moment.

## Honeymoon

The next Jasmin and I had finally arrived in the beautiful Mayan Rivera in Mexico. We were eager to start exploring the stunning beaches, take in the views of the crystal blue waters, and savor the delicious cuisine the area had to offer.

When we arrived, there was a storm brewing in the Gulf of Mexico. Hurricane Ivan was approaching, and the locals were warning us to stay away from the shore. We reluctantly decided to stay put in the resort until the storm passed, so we decided to explore the towns and villages inland.

We were amazed at the stunning Mayan ruins, the lush rainforests, and the incredible views of the mountains. We explored local markets, tasted traditional dishes, and experienced the vibrant culture of the region. We also enjoyed the occasional boat ride to the uninhabited islands nearby.

As the days passed, the storm grew stronger and stronger. We could hear the wind and the rain, and we could feel the ground tremble beneath our feet. The locals told us to stay indoors, but we ventured out to watch the storm pass. We watched in awe as the wind howled and the rain lashed against the shore.

Finally, after days of destruction, the storm subsided, and the sun began to shine. We were overjoyed to be able to explore the beaches and the coastline again.

We were immediately enchanted by the vibrant colors, lively music, and warm hospitality of the local people. We spent our days lounging on the beach, exploring ancient Mayan ruins, and trying new foods and drinks.

One of the highlights of our trip was a sunset sail along the coast. We watched as the sun dipped below the horizon, painting the sky with brilliant shades of orange and pink. As the night descended, we were treated to a breathtaking display of stars and a feeling of peace that only comes from being surrounded by nature.

We also had the opportunity to participate in a traditional Mayan ceremony, where we learned about the rich cultural heritage of the region and the significant role that spirituality played in the lives of the local people.

We grew closer and fell deeper in love with each other and with the beauty of Mexico. Our honeymoon was a truly magical experience and one that we will never forget.

Even in the aftermath of the storm, we found beauty in the Mayan Rivera. The powerful waves of the ocean, the incredible views and the vibrant culture of the locals all made for an amazing experience.

There are few things as amazing as witnessing the power of nature and the resilience of the locals in the Mayan Rivera. Even in the face of destruction, Jasmin and I were able to appreciate the beauty of the place and create lasting memories.

# Chapter 9

We arrived home from our honeymoon in the feeling refreshed and invigorated. After two weeks of exploring new places, trying new foods, and making unforgettable memories, we were eager to return to our familiar surroundings and share our experiences with our loved ones.

As we walked through the door of our home, we were greeted by the warm embrace of our family and friends. They were eager to hear all about our honeymoon and to see the photos and souvenirs we had brought back with us.

Over the next few days, we spent time catching up with everyone and sharing our favorite moments from our trip. We also took the time to unpack, sort through our photos, and start settling back into our routine.

Despite the excitement of our honeymoon and the thrill of being back home, there was a sense of sadness that lingered in the air. We had grown so close during our trip and had formed a deep connection with the people and places we had encountered.

However, as time passed and we adapted to our new lives together, we realized that the memories and experiences from our honeymoon would always be a part of us. And we were grateful for the opportunity to have shared such a special and meaningful experience.

Now as a happy married couple, my wife and I were truly the adventurous type we love to take trips. This was definitely a goal and dream of ours was to travel. We were going to make it happen plus it was something we both are passionate about. We decided we were going to go take some trips around America. We both had the flexibility in our schedules to work and travel so we took advantage to add so more adventure in our marriage. She finished her Masters and I was in my last semester so I was had to the ability to make my classes on online which I loved.

We decided our first would be San Francisco, we were so excited when we started planning our trip to the Bay Area. We had both heard of the city's reputation as a vibrant, exciting place and wanted to see it for ourselves. After a few weeks of planning, we were finally on our way.

When we arrived, we were immediately taken in by the beauty of the Bay Area. We took in the sights of the Golden Gate Bridge, and stopped to marvel at the beauty of Alcatraz Island. We spent the day strolling along the Embarcadero, exploring the many shops and restaurants. We sampled some of the local seafood and enjoyed the sounds of the street performers.

The next day, we drove around the Bay Area, taking in all the sights. We spent the day in Berkeley, enjoying a leisurely lunch in the sunshine and exploring the University of California campus. We also ventured further north, discovering stunning coastal views at Muir Beach and stunning cliffs at Point Reyes.

On our last day of our trip, we decided to take a ferry ride around the Bay. We sailed past Oakland, with its towering bridges, and peeked at the Angel Island, where Alcatraz used to be. We watched the sun set over the bay, with the colors of the sky reflecting off the choppy waters.

The trip to San Francisco was even better than we had imagined. The beauty and culture of the Bay Area had left us with unforgettable memories. We still talk about our trip whenever we see pictures of the city, reminding us of how wonderful it is to explore a new and exciting place.

Her and I always had a love and a passion for travel and travel was strengthening our bond. The power of sharing common interest is beautiful but also the power of having differences that help you grow and make each other better is important too. My wife is teaching me things about life and helping me look at things from a completely different horizon. As we would travel and do things, she would introduce me to food that I would never thought I would ever try.

On our next adventure we planned to go on a road trip to Lake Tahoe and Reno Nevada for a while. We had heard so many wonderful things about the area, and we were both really excited to explore and experience the natural beauty of the area.

Finally, we set out on our trip, leaving early in the morning, and taking in the picturesque scenery as we drove on the winding mountain roads. We made countless stops along the way, taking pictures of the stunning views and enjoying the wilderness. As we reached Lake Tahoe, we were mesmerized by its crystal-clear waters and the snow-capped mountains in the background.

With the energy of the lake and its surrounding nature, we decided to take a hike to get even closer to the lake. As we followed the path, we were in awe of the breathtaking views, and the opportunity to explore the hidden areas of the lake. We camped out under the stars, listening to the soothing sound of the lake and being mesmerized by its beauty.

In the morning, we set out for Reno, which was the perfect contrast to Lake Tahoe with its bustling city life. We explored the city, taking in the sights and sounds of the city. From the casinos to the restaurants, we had a wonderful time, and the nightlife was the perfect end to our road trip.

In the end, our trip to Lake Tahoe and Reno was a memorable experience, and we were thrilled with our decision to take the road less traveled. We made memories that will last a lifetime and enjoyed every second of our adventure.

## Windy City

I was excited to return back to the Windy City, this time I was going to experience it differently than when I was kid. I absolutely was marveled at just how beautiful Chicago is, it was like New York of the Midwest. I instantly had a connection with the city, I had never tried a Chicago deep dish pizza was definitely something on our list. So this was the city you were either a White Sox or a Cubs fan.

So as we walked into our hotel room, I am someone who absolutely loves a view, we had one of the best views you could ask for. We were just in awe and amazement in love with the view from your room. The room had floor-to-ceiling windows that offered a stunning panoramic view of the city. You could see iconic skyscrapers, bustling streets, and the sparkling lights of the city at night. One evening, we decided to order room service and have a picnic in front of the window. We spread a blanket on the floor and enjoyed a delicious meal while watching the city go by. She sipped wine and we talked late into the night, feeling grateful for the amazing experience.

The next day we decided we wanted to have lunch both had heard about the city's famous deep-dish pizza. We went to Lou Malnati's Pizzeria, and we were eager and excited to try local pizzeria experience. When the pizza arrived, we were both surprised by its size and thickness. The crust was crispy and buttery, and the toppings were fresh and abundant. We took a bite and were blown away by the explosion of flavors in your mouth. The sauce was sweet and tangy, and the cheese was gooey and melted perfectly. Jasmin and I both couldn't stop talking about how delicious that pizza was and how it was unlike anything you had ever tried before.

After that experience we were certainly anxious wanted to explore what else the Windy City had to offer.

The next day we decided to spend the day walking around and getting to know the city. We strolled down the Magnificent Mile, the main thoroughfare of Chicago, taking in the sights, sounds, and smells of the city. We stopped to admire the architecture, the skyscrapers that dominated the skyline, and the gorgeous views of Lake Michigan.

We explored the city's many parks, stopping to take a break on the steps of the Art Institute of Chicago, admiring the stunning artworks and sculptures. We made our way to Millennium Park, where we watched street performers put on a show and enjoyed the peacefulness of the lake and the city skyline.

After a full day of exploration, we took the time to relax and appreciate the beauty of the city during the night. From the observation deck of the Willis Tower, we could see the twinkling lights of the city and the stars in the sky.

After spending a few days, we had a newfound appreciation for the beauty of the city. We had explored the Windy City and made some incredible memories along the way.

## Big Apple

Our next trip, we decided to head to New York City in the summer of 2005. The city was alive with energy and excitement, and we quickly fell in love with the bustling streets and diverse cultures.

We visited iconic landmarks like the Statue of Liberty, the Empire State Building and Times Square, and we enjoyed the vibrant culture of Brooklyn and all the amazing sights that Manhattan had to offer. The energy of the city was infectious, and we could feel the history of the city with every step we took.

We spent most of our time exploring the city and trying out all of the delicious food. We tried some of the best pizza and bagels New York had to offer, and we wandered the streets in search of the best street food. Everywhere we went, there was a unique and intriguing culture that seemed to be infused into the city itself.

We also visited some of the world-famous art galleries and museums, such as the Museum of Modern Art, the American Museum of Natural History, and the Guggenheim. Everywhere we went, there was something amazing to behold, and each place we visited seemed to have its own unique story.

Our trip to New York City was the most unforgettable experience of our lives. Despite being a city of hustle and bustle, it had a unique charm and energy that we will never forget. We'll always remember the amazing sights, the incredible sounds, and the unforgettable tastes of New York City.

I planned a special date for us in Central Park and have a romantic evening together. I wanted to make it memorable, so I made reservations at Tavern on the Green, one of the most romantic restaurants in New York City.

As we entered the restaurant, we were both taken aback by the stunning interior design and the charming ambiance. The warm lighting, the flowers on the table, and the soft music created a romantic and intimate atmosphere that made us both feel like you were the only people in the room.

We were seated at a table by the window, which overlooked Central Park. The view was breathtaking, and we both took a moment to appreciate the beauty of the park at night.

As waiter approached the table and presented you with the menu. We decided to start with a glass of champagne to toast to our love and the time we had spent together. I ordered us some appetizers to share, including the lobster bisque and the shrimp cocktail. For the main course, you chose the filet mignon, while Jasmin chose the salmon.

As you enjoyed your meal, you reminisced about your journey together, recalling some of the happy memories we had shared. We laughed and joked, enjoying each other's company as much as the delicious food.

After dinner, she mostly indulged in a decadent dessert of chocolate mousse, which was the perfect sweet ending to the evening. We took a romantic stroll through Central Park, holding hands and talking about our future together.

As we were walking through the streets headed back our hotel, we stumbled upon a group of street performers who were putting on a breakdancing show. Jasmin and I couldn't resist, and but enjoy the entertainment. We both had a chuckle from the experience.

As the sun started to set, we decided to take a romantic stroll through the city. But as we were walking, a pigeon flew by and dropped a present on Jasmin's shoulder. We both started to laugh so hard that we couldn't stop, and before we knew it, we were attracting a crowd of curious onlookers.

When we returned to our hotel in New York City, we couldn't help but feel a sense of euphoria after spending the night exploring the city together.

We were reminiscing from the romantic dinner in the heart of the city, and it was a magical evening filled with laughter, delicious food, and love.

As we entered the hotel room, Jasmin took my hand and led me to the balcony to the window that overlooked the city skyline. She wrapped her arms around me and nestled her head against your chest, taking in the breathtaking view.

The sound of the city echoed in the distance, but in that moment, the only thing that mattered was the love that the two of us shared. I could feel the warmth of her embrace, the gentle rise and fall of her chest, and the tenderness of her touch.

I took a deep breath and looked out at the city, feeling grateful for the moment and the incredible woman by your side. I turned to her, looking into her eyes and taking her hand in yours.

Without a word, we both knew what was coming next. I leaned in and kissed her, and in that moment, it was as if time stood still. I could feel her lips against mine, the softness of her skin, and the warmth of her breath.

It was a moment that I would never forget. There was something special about New York City that had brought us even closer. In that moment, it was as if nothing else existed except the two of you and the love that you shared.

As I pulled away from the kiss, I looked at her and smiled, feeling as if I had just fallen in love all over again.

## City of Brotherly Love

Jasmin and I were always up for a new adventure, and so when you heard about all the amazing things to see and do in Philadelphia, we knew we had to plan a weekend trip to explore this historic city.

When we arrived in Philadelphia on a Friday afternoon and immediately headed to our hotel in the heart of the city. From there, we set out to explore all that the city had to offer.

Our first stop was Independence Hall, where you learned about the important events that took place there during the birth of the nation. We were both struck by the significance of the building and the powerful history that it represented.

We had heard about the city's famous Philly cheese steak sandwich. Then we decided to head to Pat's King of Steaks, one of the most iconic cheesesteak restaurants in the city.

When we arrived, you were greeted by a long line of people waiting to order. We felt a little intimidated but excited to try the sandwich. When we finally made it to the counter, and the server asked you what you wanted on your cheese steak. We decided to go with the classic version: thin-sliced grilled steak topped with melted cheese and served on a soft hoagie roll.

When the sandwich arrived, you both took a bite, and our taste buds were in heaven. The tender steak and melted cheese melded together, creating a perfect balance of flavors and textures. The soft hoagie roll was the perfect vessel for the delicious filling.

Jasmin and I both were blown away by the taste of the Philly cheese steak. We both agreed that it was one of the best sandwiches we had ever had and so glad we made the effort to try it. Leaving Pat's King of Steaks with full bellies and happy memories.

The next day, we visited the Liberty Bell, a symbol of American independence that I had studied about in history class. I was even amazed at how well-preserved the bell was, and you took lots of photos to remember this special moment.

In the evening, we made a stop to Reading Terminal Market, a bustling indoor market that was filled with vendors selling everything from fresh produce to artisanal cheeses. Enjoying sampling all the different foods and drinks, while loving the bustling atmosphere of the market.

On the last day of our trip, visiting the Franklin Institute, a science museum that was both educational and fun. Intrigued by the interactive exhibits, and we learned a lot about science and technology in a fun and engaging way.

Before you headed back home, decided to walk through the beautiful Fairmount Park, which we admired the stunning views of the city. Philadelphia was an amazing city, filled with history, culture, and natural beauty, and you vowed to return one day to explore more of what this vibrant city had to offer.

We left Philadelphia with a sense of wonder and a newfound appreciation for all that this historic city had to offer, and that the weekend exploring the city would always be a cherished memory.

Virginia

This was incredibly special to me, not only because it was my home state and where I grew up, but I had immense pride of being a Virginian and being part of a state that is deeply enriched in so much history. As a kid history was one of my favorite subjects. I would hear about Monticello the home of Thomas Jefferson, Jamestown, Yorktown British conceited during the

Revolutionary War, and Appomattox Courthouse where Robert E Lee and Ulysses S Grant met to end the Civil War. Also the home of the 1st president of the United States. I wanted to show Jasmin all of these different places and she was deeply intrigued to explore because of the excitement and enthusiasm of me telling these stories.

We took a road trip back to my hometown and I wanted to show her Blacksburg and the surrounding areas. I wanted to show her some of the hangout spots I used to go to. So one of the places we stopped at was a place called the hokie house. I love their food, and then next door I showed her the Barber Shop I used to go to when I was a kid to get my haircut. To my surprise my barber was still there he was still there cutting hair. Next, we drove over and I took her and showed her the New River one of the oldest rivers and the country. I showed her where my father and I used to go fishing when I was a kid. One of the special places that I took her was Mountain Lake, why this place was so special not only was it near where I grew up but it's where they filmed the movie Dirty Dancing.

Then we drove to the beautiful Blue Ridge Mountains, where you were both amazed by the stunning natural beauty of the area. We hiked along some of the trails and took in the breathtaking views of the rolling hills and the lush forests.

After a few days in the mountains, we headed to the coast, where we explored the charming seaside towns of Virginia Beach and Norfolk. We both loved the relaxed atmosphere of these towns and the opportunities for outdoor recreation like fishing and swimming.

On our way to the coast, we stopped by historic city of Richmond, we both learned about the important events that took place during the Civil War. We both were impressed by the beautiful monuments and memorials dedicated to the soldiers who fought and died during this difficult time in our country's history.

Throughout our trip, we were struck by the rich history and natural beauty of Virginia, and felt a strong connection to this beautiful state. We left the trip with a newfound appreciation for all that Virginia had to offer, and knew that you would always cherish the memories of your travels there.

From exploring the cities to admiring the natural beauty, Jasmin and I had an amazing time discovering all that my home state of Virginia had to offer.

## United Kingdom

One day I was arriving home from work my wife tells me I need you to renew your passport. I went and put in an order at the post office to get my passport updated. I had no idea what she was thinking or planning but it's always something exciting and I trust her judgment I know I'm going to have some fun. She finally surprises me and tells me we are going to go to London and have Christmas together. Coming from a small town as you know me thinking about spending Christmas in a completely different country was so foreign to me. The fear of the unknown started creeping in my mind. I was also excited because I get to learn and explore her mother's culture and heritage of growing up in the United Kingdom.

It was Christmas time, and I was about to embark on my first international trip leaving North America to London. We had talked about it for months after getting my passport renewed, and the excitement was palpable. When the day of the trip finally arrived, I threw on my best winter outfit and packed my suitcase.

I was so eager to explore all that London had to offer. Also this was another opportunity for me to get to know more about her family history since her mother was from the UK.

As we flew across the ocean, we talked and laughed, time seemingly passing in an instant.

We arrived at Heathrow airport, I slowly was just taking in every moment our first time being outside of North American soil. As a kid I always dreamed of this moment from watching the Travel Channel growing up but now this moment has finally arrived it was so surreal. My wife was looking at me she knew exactly how I was thinking and feeling because I had told her how I look forward to traveling and seeing the world. I looked at her like the travel aficionado that she was coming from such a very cultured family she knew in that moment how special and hopped into a cab I was so shocked that I'm riding in a cab where they are driving on the complete opposite side of the road than what I'm used to driving in America. The cab driver had such a very thick British accent, and I absolutely loved it. With my deep fascination for cultures, I wanted to learn everything about him. My wife planned the entire itinerary of this trip I didn't even know where we were staying or what I was going to see.

The cab pulls up in front of this very unique building and I slowly got out of the cab and just did like a 180 turn and looked at the entire view. She found a flat for us to stay in that was by the River Thames and I could see Parliament from where we were staying. I was so not ready to go in and check us in. I wanted to stay outside and take pictures, right where I was standing, I could see Big Ben and the London Eye. I simply could not believe this small-town man growing up not even seeing a traffic light in my town is seeing things that you only would think of seeing on television but it's absolute reality in this very moment.

My wife walks up to me, and she asked me what are you thinking? Is it what you expected? I told her no I could not have wanted to experience this moment with anyone else. Thank you so much, she was like well let's go inside and get something to eat and get settled in. I loved our flat, I had to get used to saying that and not say apartment. I was simply quite fascinated at how small the lift was going up to get to our flat. Once we unpacked and got settled, she gave me a brief overview of the itinerary. I was so excited I could barely eat. I thought I was going to be jet lagged but I slept so well on the flight. We showered and changed got ready and to head out and do some exploring.

The first place she takes me was as we walk down the street a little bit and she's like we're going to catch the tube. I was definitely fascinated and intrigued this was my very first time ever taking public transportation. I never robe public transportation in the DMV, so as we got our ticket and the tube slowly approached. I was shocked at how low the ceiling was and how small and I'm a very big guy. People were staring at me like I was an X-men, my wife loved it she just looked at me like her big old teddy bear. When we arrived at our stop, I realize we were at Green Park which was so beautiful in the middle of the city and she was walking escorting me around to all the places she knew. We were capturing so many different photos and then we walked over to Buckingham Palace. It was incredibly regal as soon as my eyes saw it just looking at how beautiful the gate was and also the palace itself I told her we have to get plenty of pictures.

The snow was beginning to fall and the air felt crisp with the cold. I had never seen anything like it before the city was so grand; red double-decker buses, bustling streets with people of all kinds and the River Thames flowing through it all. We decided to take a ride on the famous London Eye and take in the incredible views of the city from the top.

We were both were eager to try the local cuisine and explore the city's vibrant food scene. After a few days of trying different restaurants, we stumbled upon a quaint little bistro that quickly became your favorite place to eat in London.

The bistro was cozy and warm, with soft lighting and charming decor. The menu was filled with classic British dishes, but with a contemporary twist. We both decided to try the traditional roast beef dinner with all the trimmings, and you were not disappointed.

The beef was cooked to perfection, juicy and flavorful. The roasted vegetables were crisp and aromatic, and the gravy was rich and savory. The meal was the perfect comfort food, perfect for a chilly winter evening.

We had tickets to visit Stonehenge, one of the most famous ancient structures in the world, as part of a guided tour. We were so excited to explore this ancient wonder, but on the day of the tour, we were in for a surprise. We had overslept! We had meant to set our alarm clocks but had completely forgotten. By the time we realized what had happened, it was too late. The tour had already left without us.

We were so disappointed, but we eventually found something to laugh about. We imagined how it would have been if we had made it on the tour - the guide would have been so perplexed to see us arrive so late. We agreed that it was a good thing we hadn't made it in time, otherwise we might have been kicked out for our tardiness.

Despite this little mishap, we had the best time exploring London. We even managed to visit Stonehenge in the end, although it wasn't part of a guided tour. We took lots of pictures and enjoyed learning about the history of the ancient site. It was a trip we'll never forget!

Jasmin and I had never seen a musical together before, so when we decided to take a trip to London to watch Sweeney Todd, I was both excited and nervous. We both had butterflies in our stomachs as the lights dimmed and the curtain rose.

The first scene was a bit dark and gory, but Jasmin and I found ourselves laughing at the absurdity of it all. We were both mesmerized by the music, the sets, and the amazing singing and dancing. After the show was over, we stepped outside and marveled at the beauty of London at night.

We decided to take a night-time stroll through the city, and at one point, we ended up at a bridge, with the Thames shimmering beneath us. Jasmin said to me, "This is like something out of a fairytale!"

I replied, "Yes, it is, and we're the main characters, living a wonderful adventure."

We spent the rest of the night talking about our experience and reflecting on the show. We had made a memory that we would never forget. We both agreed that a Sweeney Todd tour of London was one of the most memorable and enjoyable experiences we had ever had.

From that moment forward I was absolutely in utopia I wanted to explore the rest of what this place had to offer. When we went over to Piccadilly Circus I was like wow this is like a another time square. You know Camden lock reminded me of canal street when I visited New York with my father as a kid. You know when you read and see these fascinating places on TV I realize it doesn't do it justice until you see it and live it in person. London taught me how much I wanted to see the rest of the world I wanted to connect with so many other places the way I'm connecting with where I'm at right now. It was euphoria occasion because I am living my dream that I never thought would be possible. At the end of our trip as we were packing our bags and heading back to the states, I felt motivated and inspired I wanted to take our lives to the next level.

The rest of the trip was filled with more sight-seeing, shopping and savoring the city's delicious food. I tried my best to take in every moment, to savor all the experiences I was having, for I knew I would never forget this trip. Throughout the trip, Jasmin acted as my personal tour guide, she showed me her favorite places and gave me her own personal insights.

My first international trip abroad to London with Jasmin was an extraordinary experience and one that I will never forget. From the moment we arrived until the moment we said goodbye, I felt a deep sense of appreciation for being able to visit this amazing city. Taking a trip of a lifetime with a special someone made it even more meaningful.

Careers

Jasmin had always been driven and dedicated, with a passion for her work and a strong work ethic. Throughout her career, she worked hard to hone her skills, expand her knowledge, and build relationships with her colleagues and clients.

However, despite her best efforts, her career seemed to be stuck in a rut. She felt as though her progress was stagnating and that her hard work was going unnoticed.

One day, everything changed. Jasmin received an exciting opportunity to take on a new project that would challenge her in ways she never imagined. She jumped at the chance and threw herself into the work, determined to prove her worth and make the most of this chance.

Her challenging work paid off. The project was a resounding success and Jasmin's contributions were recognized and celebrated by her colleagues and clients. Word of her success spread quickly and she was soon in high demand, with new opportunities and offers coming in from all directions.

As her career took off, Jasmin was amazed at how far she had come and how much she had accomplished. She was grateful for the opportunities she had been given and for the support of her friends, family, and colleagues.

With each new challenge she faced, Jasmin grew stronger and more confident. She continued to push herself, to take risks, and to pursue her passions with a sense of purpose and determination.

Even with the busy hectic work of our careers we still always made time to travel and do things that we love that continue to bond us and grow our connection.

Travel Challenges

Jasmin and I will never forget the flight from DC to Chicago. We were both looking forward to the trip, but what we didn't expect was the reaction of the passengers around us.

As soon as we boarded the plane and took our seats, people started to take notice of our height. We both stand over 6 feet tall, and the small seats and cramped quarters on the plane made it clear that we were going to be a bit of a spectacle.

The flight attendants kept coming over to check on us, making sure that we were comfortable and had enough room. People kept pointing and whispering, and we couldn't help but feel like celebrities.

At one point, a woman leaned over to us and asked if we were basketball players. We couldn't contain our laughter and told her that we were just tall people on their way to Chicago.

The flight went by quickly as we made new friends with our seatmates, who were all entertained by our height and the attention that we were getting.

We arrived in Chicago feeling refreshed and rejuvenated, and with a funny story to tell. From that day on, we always joke about how we were famous on that flight and how we will never forget the time that we felt like celebrities in the sky.

## Atlanta

Traveling back to Atlanta brought back some nostalgic memories that I had as a kid with my father as one of our road trips. My father and I were huge Atlanta Braves fans as a kid we used to love watching I love that Dave Justice, Fred McGriff, Greg Maddux and John Smoltz.

When Jasmin  and I arrived we decided we were going to get a rental car to drive around and explore. I had never thought we were going to get lost as often as we did while trying to explore. Every street in Atlanta was named Peachtree, and then when we asked for directions it sounded even more confusing. It seemed like there was a Waffle House on every corner. I kept asking myself how did my father do it when I was a kid he made it seem so effortless, my father had a strong sense of navigation. He could find dirt in a snowstorm if you asked him to.

We were laughing hysterically in the car our first day trying to drive around and I kept asking her did we pass that Waffle House or is that a different one.

Once we got our bearings together, we ended up having a blast. It was Friday afternoon, and we finally found our hotel in the heart of the city. From there, we set out to explore all that Atlanta had to offer.

Our first stop was the Martin Luther King Jr. National Historic Site, we learned about the life and legacy of this important civil rights leader. You both were struck by the significance of this site and the powerful messages of hope and equality that it represented.

Next, we visited the High Museum of Art, where you admired the stunning works of art on display. Jasmin was so fascinated by the different styles and techniques that the artists used, and you loved the opportunity to learn more about art and culture.

In the evening, we headed to the trendy neighborhood of Midtown, where you enjoyed a delicious meal at a local restaurant and strolled through the streets, taking in the sights and sounds of this vibrant area.

The next day we visited the famous World of Coca-Cola, we learned about the history and culture of this iconic brand. You both loved the interactive exhibits and the fun, playful atmosphere of the museum.

After exploring the city, you decided to take a trip to the suburbs to see a different side of Atlanta. You visited the charming town of Roswell, where you walked along the riverfront and admired the beautiful homes and gardens.

Before you headed back home, you took a drive along the scenic highways, admiring the rolling hills and stunning scenery that surrounded you.


Jamaica

We were eager to escape the daily grind and to soak up the sun, sand, and sea of this vibrant island nation. We were staying in the beautiful resort town of Runaway Bay, renowned for its crystal-clear waters and lush tropical landscapes.

As soon as we stepped out of the airport, it was such a humbling experience. we were immediately struck by the beauty of your surroundings and the warmth of the local people.  As we begin riding and our taxi on the way to the resort I was completely mesmerized at how many people were just walking along the streets and this seemed to be the main highway. The driver was telling us that some of the houses that we would see we're not even finished being built because some of the projects just ran out of money.

My heart instantly really connected with the culture there despite some of the conditions I had never seen people that were just so high spirited about just living their life.

As the staff were taking our bags to our rooms I decided to just walk around the resort. This was our first time being at a resort that had a nude side and prude side. There were people literally walking around totally nude just free letting it all hang out. If you could imagine the look on our face, we chuckled. I was curious to just walk over to the nude side, I stopped at the bar I wanted to just get a bottle of water. All of a sudden, I hear these ladies yelling "take it off" and I turned around they were yelling at me to remove all my clothing. Never have I ever had a woman yell at me to remove my clothing before I was flattered and perplexed all in the same moment.

Then the management walks over to me and says "Sir if you're going to be on this side you cannot have on any clothes."

I immediately took a sip of my water and walked back over to the prude side I wasn't ready to reveal to the world what I had to offer.

Each day was filled with adventure and excitement, from early morning yoga classes on the beach to snorkeling expeditions through the turquoise waters. We visited local markets and sampled delicious Jamaican cuisine, from spicy jerk chicken to sweet, juicy pineapple.

I booked us a take a tour of Jamaica from our resort in Runaway Bay. The tour began with a drive through "Ocho Rios," where we were able to see some of the stunning sights and natural beauty of the island. We then continued to Negril, taking in the stunning vistas and vibrant atmosphere of the Caribbean.

Then friendly tour guide who showed us around and shared interesting facts about the island. The famous Dunn's River Falls, where you can climb the 600-foot waterfall or take a dip in the refreshing pools at the bottom.

We sampled the famous Jerk Chicken stands, where we tried the famous Jamaican dish, cooked over a smoky fire with a blend of spices and seasonings. The flavor was a unique blend of heat and sweetness, and it was delicious!

We had lunch in Negril, known for its stunning Seven Mile Beach. We spent the afternoon soaking up the sun and playing in the crystal-clear water. Even went snorkeling and saw colorful fish and coral in the turquoise waters. We got to explore the amazing Seven Mile Beach and the town of Negril. We marveled at the spectacle of the cliffs at Negril Point.

The tour ended with a visit to a local rum distillery, where we learned about the process of making rum and got to sample different flavors. Then finished the day with a beautiful sunset over the ocean, a perfect ending to a wonderful day in Jamaica.

In the evenings, we would take long walks along the beach, watching as the sun set over the Caribbean and the stars twinkled above. We sipped cocktails at open-air bars and danced to the sounds of live reggae music, fully embracing the laid-back lifestyle of this island paradise.

After taking in the sights, we spent the remainder of the day relaxing and enjoying the beach.

Throughout the trip, Jasmin and I grew closer, relishing the time spent together and making new memories that would last a lifetime.

Tall People Problems

We often found ourselves struggling to get comfortable on flights because of our height and long legs. The cramped seats and limited legroom on most airplanes made it difficult for us to stretch out and relax during long flights.

We tried everything to find a solution, from booking seats with extra legroom to carrying inflatable footrests and bringing our own pillows. No matter what we did, it always felt like we were fighting a losing battle.

On our long-haul flight from DC to San Francisco we were seated in separate rows. When we finally arrived at our destination, we were both exhausted and uncomfortable from being cramped up in our seats for hours.

That's when we decided enough was enough, and we started researching airlines that offered more legroom for tall passengers. To our surprise, we found several airlines that cater to people with longer legs and more spacious seating arrangements.

From then on, whenever we travel, we make sure to book our flights on these airlines, and it has made all the difference. Now, we can sit back and relax on flights, knowing that we have plenty of room to stretch out and be comfortable.

We learned that a little research and planning goes a long way, especially when it comes to making sure we have a comfortable and stress-free travel experience.

## Shopping for Clothes

We often struggled when it came to finding clothes that fit our tall and athletic build while we were traveling. It seemed like everywhere we went, the clothes were either too short or too tight in all the wrong places.

On our trip to London and we were both in desperate need of new outfits for a special event. We went from store to store, but everything seemed to be either too small or too short for us.

We even tried shopping at some of the high-end boutiques, but still, nothing seemed to fit. It was as if the clothing industry had never heard of tall and athletic people before.

We were starting to get frustrated and discouraged, but Jasmin refused to give up. She was determined to find something that would fit us both and make us feel confident and stylish.

After hours of searching, we finally found a store that specialized in clothing for people with our build. The clothes were not only a perfect fit, but they were also fashionable and stylish.

From that day on, whenever we travel, we always make a point to go to that store and stock up on clothes that fit us perfectly. It's no longer a struggle to find clothes that fit our unique bodies, and we can now travel in comfort and style.

At times, when Jasmin and I travel together, people kept mistaking us for famous athletes. Since we both have a strong and athletic build, and people couldn't help but stare at us wherever we went.

It all started when we were walking through the airport, and people kept stopping us to ask for autographs. They thought that I was a NFL football player because of my height and build, and they were shocked when I told them that I wasn't.

The same thing happened when we were at the hotel in Chicago. They were convinced that we were famous athletes and the shocked look on the faces when said no we weren't was hysterical.

We found the whole experience quite amusing, and we couldn't help but laugh at the reactions of the people around us. We felt like celebrities, even though we were just normal people on a trip together.

As the days went on, people continued to mistake us for famous athletes, and we couldn't help but enjoy the attention. We even started to play along and signed autographs for people, just for fun.

# Chapter 10

It was a Saturday afternoon I sat down at the dining room table writing down some new goals that I think my wife and I can accomplish. We were outgrowing our current living situation and I said to her I think it's time for us to explore the option of buying a home.

She had finished her master's degree and I finished my bachelors. No longer working two jobs to get through school, we were doing quite well financially but we were modest people and always living below our means. Another reason that allowed us to be able to travel a lot.

She was definitely intrigued at where my mind was going, and she asked me do you think we're ready to take on the financial responsibilities of owning a home. I always loved that I could present anything to her she wouldn't immediately shoot it down but she would challenge my level of thought to see if I've thought about everything.

Jasmin sat down with me to talk about the kind of home she envisioned us living in. She shared with me her dreams of a cozy, welcoming home with plenty of natural light and a big, beautiful garden. She talked about the importance of having a place where we could entertain friends and family, and where we could spend time together as a couple.

I listened intently as she spoke, and I was struck by the passion and excitement in her voice. I could tell that this was something that was important to her, and I wanted to make sure that we found the perfect home together.

I was very ambitious ready to take on some new challenges accomplish some new goals personally and professionally. I was so proud of her she had just landed a new executive opportunity. So we beginning exploring the options of owning a home. Deciding on what type of home we wanted to live in and at this time the housing market was like 7 to 9 buyers for every seller. So it was very competitive but I've learned in life that anything worth having doesn't come easy.

Luckily, her sister was in finance, and she was able to give us some great options on the type of mortgage that we could go for.

As we went through the home buying process, we both learned a great deal about what to look for in a property and how to navigate the world of real estate. We also learned the importance of working together as a team and supporting each other through the ups and downs of the journey.

Meeting with our realtor

Jasmin and I walk into the realtor's office and are greeted by a friendly, yet slightly eccentric realtor. He seemed to be quite nervous, he immediately launches into a monologue about the local real estate market and all of the exciting properties they have to offer. Jasmin and I exchange a confused look and nod politely as the realtor continues to speak at a rapid-fire pace.

Just as the realtor takes a breath, Jasmin knew to crack a few jokes to lighten the mood and asks, "So, are any of these properties haunted by friendly ghosts or do we have to worry about any poltergeists?"

The realtor chuckles nervously and assures us that none of the properties are haunted, but he does have a few stories about strange occurrences in some of the older homes. Jasmin and I exchange another look but decide to go ahead with the tour anyway.

He started to relax, and then he goes on to show Jasmin and I a variety of properties, but every time the realtor starts to get serious, Jasmin brings up another absurd request, like a property with a trampoline room or a tree house. By the end of the meeting, the realtor is in stitches and Jasmin and I are feeling more relaxed and at ease.

We spent countless hours looking at homes, both online and in person. Jasmin was always the one to point out the little details that made each home special, and she always had a vision for how we could make each one our own.

So, we found an amazing home in Southern Maryland, four-bedroom 2 bath had a with a pool in the backyard. A great place for our friends to come over our family could spend the night we were just ecstatic of starting a new life together.

Despite the obstacles, Jasmin and I were determined to make the purchase happen. We spent countless hours researching the property, speaking with real estate agents, and gathering information to make an informed decision.

Day of Closing

We arrived at the title company's office, ready to sign all of the necessary paperwork to close on our first home. The room is filled with stacks of papers and the title agent starts going over each document one by one.

As we sign each page, the title agent starts to pile the signed papers into a neat stack on the table. Jasmin and I are feeling a bit overwhelmed by the sheer volume of paperwork they have to sign.

Just as we're getting into the rhythm of signing and stacking, the title agent hands us a particularly long document. Jasmin and I start signing it, but as we get to the end, we realize that we signed on top of each other's signatures!

The title agent looks at the page, then up at Jasmin and then looked at me, and starts to laugh. "Don't worry, it happens all the time," the title agent says, trying to stifle a chuckle.

Even in a serious situation like closing on a home, it's important to maintain a lighthearted attitude and not get too bogged down by the details. Sometimes, a little laughter can make a big difference.

In the end, we found the perfect home. It was everything that Jasmin had envisioned and more. We were both so happy to have found a place to call our own and to start making memories together.

Jasmin's passion and dedication to finding the perfect home inspired me, and I will always be grateful to her for sharing her vision with me and for making it a reality, truly another dream come true for us and we made it happen.

Jasmin and I were over the moon when we finally found our dream home.

We spent hours touring the property, imagining ourselves living there and creating memories with our friends and family. When the time finally came to make an offer, we were so excited that we couldn't contain our nerves.

We went through the buying process with ease, and before we knew it, we were the proud owners of a new home. The first thing we did was invite all of our friends over to celebrate and break in the pool. It was the perfect way to start our new life together.

We had just moved into our new home and we were eager to explore our new surroundings. As we walked around the house, we noticed that we had a lot of unpacking to do. We decided to take a break and head outside for a little bit of fresh air.

As we stepped outside, we were greeted by the warm sunshine and the gentle breeze. The neighborhood was quiet and peaceful, with friendly neighbors occasionally walking their dogs. We decided to take a walk around the block to get a better sense of our new community.

As we walked, we noticed the beautiful trees and well-manicured lawns of the houses. We also stumbled upon a local park, where children were playing, and families were having picnics. We stopped to take in the scenery and couldn't help but feel grateful for our new home and the community we had just become a part of.

After our walk, we returned to our house feeling refreshed and energized. We tackled the unpacking with renewed enthusiasm, excited to make our new house feel like home. We knew that there would be more exploring to do in the coming days and weeks, but for now, we were content with the simple pleasures of a quiet neighborhood walk and the promise of a new beginning.

As we began to settle in, we spent our weekends painting and decorating, making the house truly our own. Jasmin found the perfect pieces of furniture to decorate each room, and we both loved spending time in the backyard by the pool.

On one particularly warm weekend, we invited some friends over for a pool party. As we swam and laughed, we couldn't help but feel grateful for our new home and the memories we were already making there.

As the sun began to set, we fired up the grill and prepared a delicious meal for our guests. We sat around the table, chatting and enjoying each other's company. It was a perfect evening, and we couldn't help but feel grateful for our new community and the wonderful friends we had made.

As our guests left and we cleaned up the backyard, Jasmin turned to me and said, "I can't believe how lucky we are to have this home and these friends."

I agreed, and we both took a moment to appreciate the little moments that make life so special.

As we went to bed that night, we both felt a sense of contentment and happiness that we knew would only grow as we continued to build a life in our new home.

Finally, after months of hard work and determination, we were able to close on the house and move in. We were overjoyed to finally have a place to call our own and to start making memories in our new home.

From that day forward, Jasmin and I continued to work together on maintaining and improving our home.

Housewarming Party

Thrilled to be hosting our first housewarming party in our new four-bedroom, two-bathroom house with a pool in the backyard. Jasmin took on the task of preparing for the party with eagerness and excitement.

Days before the party, Jasmin could be found in the kitchen cooking up a storm. She wanted to impress our friends and family with her culinary skills, so she prepared an array of delicious foods and drinks. From juicy hamburgers and hot dogs to fresh fruit salads and homemade dips, she had it all covered.

Jasmin also spent hours decorating the house to make it look its best. She created beautiful centerpieces for the table, hung balloons and streamers, and set up a cozy seating area by the pool.

The day of the party, Jasmin was a whirlwind of activity, making sure everything was just right. She greeted each guest with a warm smile and made sure they had everything they needed. As the guests arrived, they were in awe of the beautiful home and all of the delicious food.

As the party got into full swing, Jasmin took a moment to sit back and enjoy the festivities. She was proud of the work she had put into making the housewarming party a success and grateful for all of the love and support of our friends and family.

Jasmin's hard work and dedication to making the party perfect paid off, and it was a day that will always be remembered. Our friends and family left with full bellies and happy hearts, and Jasmin and I felt grateful for the beautiful new home that we had created together.

Shortly after we got settled in our home I was getting ready for my graduation since I finished a semester early. It was such a monumental accomplishment on top of everything else but this was so special to me because I was the first one in my family to graduate from college. My mom decided to take my degree and hang it on her wall at home so she could look at it all the time. I always just wanted to make my family proud they sacrificed so much. Even though my grandparents didn't get to make it or my aunt they were there with me in spirit.

## Graduation

After years of hard work and dedication, my friends and I were finally graduating from college. We were all eager to celebrate this major accomplishment, so we decided to throw a huge graduation party.

The day of the party arrived, and my friends and I worked together to set everything up. The grill was fired up, and the delicious aroma of burgers and hot dogs filled the air.

As our guests arrived, they were greeted with cheers and excitement. We had friends and family from all over come to celebrate with us. The party was in full swing, and the energy was electric. We laughed, danced, and reminisced about our college years, and we made new memories that we'll always cherish.

Throughout the party, my friends and I took turns giving speeches, sharing memories, and thanking each other for the support and friendship we had shared throughout college. We each shared our plans for the future and talked about the exciting things we had in store.

As the night drew to a close, my friends and I stood together, proud of what we had accomplished and grateful for all the support we had received from each other. Our graduation party was a huge success, and it was a perfect way to celebrate this major milestone in our lives. I was so proud and blessed to have them as friends.

From that day forward, my friends and I will always look back on our graduation party as a special time in our lives. It was a day filled with joy, love, and memories that will last a lifetime.

## DIY Projects

First time being a homeowner, and I was excited to finally do some DIY around the house. I was determined to tackle the yard work, so I went to Home Depot to get the supplies I would need to get the job done.

It was a bit overwhelming since I had never been to Home Depot before. I had no idea where everything was and I was sure I was going to break something with all the tools I was carrying around. I started asking the employees for help and it quickly became apparent that none of them knew what I was talking about.

Finally, I spotted a middle-aged man in a Home Depot apron who seemed like he knew what he was doing. I asked him if he could help me find what I needed and he smiled and began to show me around the store.

As we went around the store, he asked me what I was doing, and when I told him I was tackling the yard work he chuckled and said, "You know, the real trick to yard work isn't the tools, it's the process. You have to take your time and plan things out, that's how you get the job done right."

I thanked him for the advice and he told me to not forget the most important tool for any project common sense! I thanked him again, got what I needed and went home to tackle the yard work.

I ended up taking his advice and took my time planning things out. In the end, I was able to get the job done and I realized that it was indeed the process, not the tools, that was most important when it came to yard work.

Jasmin was always one for sprucing up our home, she immediately had a plan to make it even more special. She went to the garden section at Home Depot planning out what she wanted to do and purchased a few flats of colorful flowers.

She began to carefully plot out where she wanted to place each flat. She dug several holes in strategic locations in the front and back yards, then carefully placed the plants in each spot.

Jasmin had planted each flower in a pattern that made it look like a work of art. The colors and shapes of the flowers had completely transformed the new house. It was at that moment I saw my grandmother in her planting flowers.

Our families and I was so delighted by Jasmin's work that they decided to take a family photo in the yard. Each member made sure to stand close to their favorite flower while they posed.

## Hurricane Katrina

Few months after graduation, I received a call from Calvin that his family was trapped in New Orleans from Hurricane Katrina.

Calvin and Peter were close friends, and when Hurricane Katrina hit, Calvin's family was stuck in New Orleans. Calvin was frantic with worry and wanted to go and rescue them, but he was afraid to go alone.

That's where Peter stepped in. He told Calvin that he would go with him to rescue his family, no matter what. They packed a car with supplies and headed to New Orleans, determined to find Calvin's family and bring them to safety.

The journey was treacherous, with flooded roads and fallen trees blocking their path. Peter and Calvin were determined, and they pushed on, relying on each other for support and encouragement.

Finally, they arrived in New Orleans and started searching for Calvin's family. The city was in chaos, with buildings and homes destroyed, but they pushed on, determined to find Calvin's family.

After what seemed like an eternity, they finally found Calvin's family, holed up in a shelter. They were exhausted, hungry, and scared, but the sight of Calvin and Peter was a welcome one.

Peter and Calvin helped Calvin's family gather their things and get into the car. They started the long journey back, this time with Calvin's family in tow. I told Calvin we have spare bedrooms if anyone wanted to stay with us.

The trip back was just as difficult as the trip there, but they finally made it to safety. Calvin's family was overjoyed to be reunited, and they hugged and thanked Peter and Calvin for their bravery and determination.

So after I had finished doing some work in the garage, my wife was setting by the fireplace and I came to join her in the living room. She asked me about, "What do you think about having children? do you think we are ready?"

The first thing that popped up in my mind was I totally understand why she would think this that would be the next goal that we should be trying to work towards. She definitely would make the perfect mom for our kids.

Jasmin and I had always talked about starting a family one day, but as we began to plan for it, we realized that we had some different ideas about what that meant. For Jasmin, having children was a top priority, and she wanted to start trying as soon as possible. On the other hand, I was a little more hesitant. I had concerns about the financial and emotional responsibility of having children, and I wanted to make sure we were both fully ready for the challenge. Plus, there was other life goals I wanted to attain before her I crossed that bridge.

Despite our differences, Jasmin and I were determined to work through our issues and find a solution that worked for both of us. We talked openly and honestly about our concerns, and we listened to each other's perspectives. We did our research and sought advice from trusted friends and family members.

One of the biggest challenges we faced was finding a balance between our life goals, careers and our plans for starting a family. Jasmin had always been focused on her career but she was at a stage where she was ready didn't want to put it on hold for motherhood. While I was a little more flexible and willing to wait until later time to start that journey.

Eventually, we reached a compromise, we agreed to wait and give it some time before trying to have children, so that we could both continue to focus on our careers, goals and build our financial security. In the meantime, we started making plans for the future, talking about different parenting styles and discussing our values and beliefs about raising children.

Through our journey, Jasmin and I learned that the process of navigating marital differences is not always easy, but it's worth it in the end. We grew as a couple, learned to listen to each other and appreciate each other's perspectives, and ultimately found a solution that worked for both of us. As we prepare for parenthood, we're confident that we're ready for the challenge ahead and that we'll be able to handle it together.

As time passed, I began to ponder the thought of having children at this stage and age in our lives, this was major if we embrace this. I absolutely love the freedom that we could travel when we wanted to and do certain things. I know that children would be our greatest legacy but that's a legacy I wasn't ready to build and commit to just yet. I felt incredibly guilty that I was feeling this way, I know this is something important that my wife is ready for and I wasn't ready to give it to her. It felt selfish but it really hurt a lot that she had given and shared with me so much. I wasn't ready to begin sharing this. I love the notion of being a husband, partner, and a best friend. When you add father to that title that's the biggest responsibility of my entire life. Another human is depending on me for their entire existence, and I had to finally come clean and be honest with her about how I was feeling. I told her that there is more I want to do in this life before I become a father there's more experiences I want to have and share with us and for myself.

This was the first time in our relationship in our marriage that I felt like a failure, the worst feeling in the world is when you feel like you disappointed the person you love so much. Being a perfectionist overthinking overanalyzing, this was something that bothered me for a while. We had talked about kids and wanting to have them when we were dating but we didn't set a timeline on it. I realized that there is an age gap between her and I we weren't the same age she's at a different age and stage of life than I was.

I learned that life is going to present numerous opportunities and numerous challenges and you've got to learn how to navigate through it all. Trying to navigate our marriage through this became a big deal for us. I had started a business along with working to build more on our financial pipeline but I had ran into several challenges and ultimately the business failed.

Starting a business is always a risk, and I learned that the hard way when my first IT consulting business failed. I had always had a passion for technology and a desire to be my own boss, so I thought that launching an IT consulting business would be the perfect opportunity to combine my two interests.

I poured my heart and soul into my business, working long hours and investing all so much time and energy. Set up a website to promote my services. At first, things were going well. We landed a few small contracts, and I was confident that we were on our way to success.

However, as time went on, it became clear that my business was not going to be as successful as I had hoped. It was hard to attract new business facing stiff competition from larger, more established consulting firms.

I started reflecting on how my father and my grandfather did it with the immense challenges that they had at my age. I always inspire to be strong like them, they made marriage looks so easy. I started envisioning different scenarios since my wife planted those seeds in my head about family.

The overanalyzing side of my brain kicked in once again, and I started thinking about what if she couldn't work and I had to provide. I know how scary it was for my father when he got sick and couldn't provide like he used to. I did not want my wife and future family going through those hardships I wanted to build a successful foundation. I looked at marriage the same way I looked at how my grandparents attended to their garden. You need a good foundation (soil) you got to water it, give it sunlight it needs but it requires constant attention meanwhile giving it all that attention it needs to grow. I want a life where my wife and family we were growing and evolving. At this stage I did not feel comfortable and secure enough within myself.

I learned in this moment that I am just not the man and husband she needs, I was letting my fears insecurities get the best of me. I was doing well in my career, but I didn't feel comfortable enough where I want it to be to start a family. For several months into our marriage this bothered me I felt like I needed to work more. My days got longer setting in traffic getting home I was exhausted. I was trying to figure out no new ways of making money. Because I watch my mom raise me and she was a stay-at-home mom a lot of the times.  I would imagine that my wife would need to do that for us at times. I started feeling like a failure and a disappointment, I'm very hard on myself I take great pride in holding myself to a high regard. I tried doing everything I could, but it felt like the universe was playing tricks on me.

At times I'd walk around at home, and I'd look in one of the guest bedrooms that I knew that could be a potential room for our future child and there were times I had set in that room and envision a little me running around. Here is another day that I have failed her, I was never that kind of person to make irrational decisions. Every major decision I made in my life I was ready for it but no matter what I did I could not get myself to be ready for this. I wasn't secure enough within myself to make that decision of becoming a father.

It was a Friday evening after a long week that my wife and I had sat down with her in the living room of our home. I shared with her what I had been thinking and feeling, I had gotten to a point I was just not happy like the way I wanted to be. It was not with our marriage it was with myself, and she asked what can I do to help?  I said to her there's nothing really you can do this is a personal battle that I'm dealing with from within. I told her I'm tired of feeling guilty that you're ready for something that I'm not ready for. I'm struggling trying to navigate finding happiness with it. This was a very major internal battle I was struggling with the woman I loved so much. I realized I was not at a comfortable point in my career to be the man she needed me to be. As a man you hate feeling like a failure especially in front of your woman it eats away at you on the inside.

I envisioned our marriage being like my grandparents I wanted to be with her and ride off into the sunset. I told her I needed to take a break I needed to spend some time with myself, looking at you in this house makes me feel guilty. I felt like I was wasting her time she's too good of a person, but I was stressed out and I couldn't think straight. I had begun packing my stuff and then I was going to work on a transition plan of where I wanted to stay I needed to spend some time alone.

# Chapter 11

Preparing for a transition once I told my wife I was going to live on my own I needed some time to just reflect. I know it sounds crazy, selfish, and stupid but at this time that was what I needed. There were personal things as a man that I needed to work on, at the time she probably thought I was being irrational, but she respected my decision. I always loved her for that even in the times when she didn't understand she supported me. She knew when to turn off being a wife and being an understanding best friend and vice versa. I know there were times she may have been sad, angry and upset but I always loved her emotional intelligence during our tough times together. I certainly lacked emotional intelligence I even struggled with empathy throughout the course of our marriage. This time in my life I was twenty-four years old, and I realized that being in my twenties this is the time my life when you're going through self-discovery of the kind of adult that you see yourself being.

This transition in my life was the hardest transition I had ever gone through up to this point. I had to walk away from the woman I love, because I knew I could not meet the needs of what she needed to be happy. Not only did I love her, but I was in love with her, I felt as if during this phase of life there is more I wanted to attain and accomplish.

Being a small-town kid getting married young was a norm from my culture, my grandparents got married when they were teenagers. My father got married when he was nineteen years old. I realized for me even though I was ready to be married and start a life there were also things about me that I wanted to explore and find out more.

I went back to Virginia for a little while stayed on my own, My wife and I we kept in touch, I always wanted to check on her. She stayed on my mind constantly, I loved it that she wasn't bitter or had no ill will towards me. The bond of our strong friendship and foundation was just immaculately special. Her family still considered me like another son I thought they would have been angry and upset with me but everyone was very supportive and understanding. They all handled it with the utmost grace, and I love them for that. Even my friends were very supportive sad but they understood.

At first it was very weird living on my own, I hadn't done it in so long but I need it time to myself. This was going to truly help me in self-reflecting on what I needed to work on for the future.

Going through a separation is never easy, and it can be especially challenging when it involves two people who once shared a home and a life together. When Jasmin and I decided to separate, we were both facing an uncertain future, and we didn't know what the transition would look like.

Jasmin and I were at different ages and stages of our life during this time, I wanted to continue to achieve a lot of personal and professional goals that I had set out for myself and so did she even though we deeply loved each other we knew it was time for us to be apart to figure things out. That love, respect, understanding, and friendship still resided is what kept us connected even though we were apart. There were times we still called each other, picked our brains about various topics not only seeing how we were doing. We both knew that we were not going to have the type of connection where we just completely severed communication and did not hear from each other. One of the things that I'm thankful for and that I always love about our connection is how pragmatic we were in our approach to life and in our relationship. We always wanted the best for each other even if we were together or not. Even though our plan for wanting to start a family didn't work out, we both learned to make peace with it so we could move forward.

Being a father is something I've always envisioned seeing myself being one day and having experiences and things that I could share and pass down to my children. I had not finished living life for myself and doing a lot of life goals before making that transition and I knew if we had started a family too soon that wouldn't have been good. Life has taught me you're going to make some tough decisions, and a lot of times those tough decisions are the ones that you may not easily want to face but you know it's the right decision. I always wanted the best for her even if it's not with me I've learned that love is not selfish it's selfless being able to put your partner's interest above your own is vital in a relationship. It was truly a blessing that we could handling going through this amicably.

A little over a year had passed since we had not been together, we both decided it was time for us to meet and talk. We had not seen each other for quite a while, and we felt there was some conversations that were better handled face to face than over the phone. So I decided that we should meet at one of our favorite places that we like to go to it was quiet and I was certain there wasn't going to be a lot of people and we could just focus.

We met at Haynes point in DC we always love that place being by the water you can get some really great views down there. I arrived a little early I was always the type that liked to be punctual or early for everything. She was running a little behind and then I saw her walk up to where I was setting. She looked stunning as always so we hugged and greeted each other then we began to sat down. You can tell we definitely had a lot that we wanted to share and talk about. I wanted her to speak first, and what she said to me completely blew me away.

Stay Tuned....Volume II.

# About the Author

Mac Harvey is as an IT Consultant Software Developer, Writer, World Traveler, Investor and Entrepreneur. Born and raised in the United States from Virginia, he has always been passionate about exploring new cultures and expanding his horizons.

Mac's interest in technology began at a young age when he started tinkering with computers and programming languages. As he grew older, he decided to pursue a career in software development and attended college to study Network and Communications Management. Prior to graduation, he landed his first internship with IBM, where he quickly rose through the ranks and became a lead developer and Project Manager within a few years.

Despite his success in the tech industry, Mac felt a strong urge to explore the world and experience different cultures. He took a sabbatical from work and spent several months traveling around the globe, immersing himself in new environments and meeting people from all walks of life. His travels inspired him to write a book about his experiences.

During his travels, Mac decided to start his own software development and IT Consulting company, leveraging his expertise and network to build a successful business from scratch.

Throughout his career, Mac has remained committed to the principles of hard work, innovation, and personal growth. He is known for his unwavering dedication to his craft, his insatiable curiosity about the world, and his boundless creativity and energy. His impact on the tech industry and the world at large is a testament to his vision and tenacity, and his legacy as a trailblazer and innovator will continue to inspire generations to come.

www.ingramcontent.com/pod-product-compliance
Lightning Source LLC
Chambersburg PA
CBHW021207160726
47994CB00001B/379